D0913121

DANCE CRITICS ASSOCIATION

LOOKING OUT

PERSPECTIVES ON DANCE AND CRITICISM IN A MULTICULTURAL WORLD

Edited by David Gere

Coeditors:

Lewis Segal
Patrice Clark Koelsch
Elizabeth Zimmer

792.8
L863

Alverno College
Library Media Center
Milwaukee, Wisconsin

Schirmer Books
An Imprint of Simon & Schuster Macmillan
New York

Prentice Hall International
London   Mexico City   New Delhi   Singapore   Sydney   Toronto

© 1995 by Dance Critics Association

All rights reserved. No part of this book may
be reproduced or transmitted in any form or by
any means, electronic or mechanical,
including photocopying, recording, or by any
information storage and retrieval system,
without permission in writing from the Publisher.

Design: Cal Anderson
Copyediting: Barbara Palfy
Proofreading: Joanne Shwed, Backspace Ink
Page Composition: Jeffrey Brandenburg, ImageComp

Schirmer Books
An imprint of Simon & Schuster Macmillan
866 Third Avenue, New York, N.Y. 10022

Library of Congress Catalog Card Number: 95-68941
ISBN: 0-02-870683-8

Printed in the United States of America
Printing Number
1   2   3   4   5   6   7   8   9   10

This paper meets the requirements of ANSI/NISO Z39.48-1992
(Permanence of Paper).

ABOUT THE DANCE CRITICS ASSOCIATION

The Dance Critics Association was founded in 1974 to promote excellence in dance criticism through education, research, and the exchange of ideas. A nonprofit institution, it is the only organization in North America devoted primarily to improving the quality of dance writing. DCA boasts an international membership of writers, broadcasters, and dance scholars, with a large complement of student members and reciprocal arrangements with organizations such as the Society of Dance History Scholars, Congress on Research in Dance, and the American Dance Guild. The Association publishes a quarterly newsletter, a directory, and other professional publications, as well as holding conferences, seminars, and other events for professional growth. To become a member or to learn more about DCA, write: Dance Critics Association, P.O. Box 1882, Old Chelsea Station, New York, New York 10011.

CIAO, COLUMBUS

Penelope tells her son
you may drink juice   don't ask for soda.
David drinks the juice.
David says I need a picture of an "Indian" for school.
Penelope tells her son
the people who were here when Columbus came
were and are   proud of their metaphoric names.
"Indian" if it does not refer to the "Indies"
east of India   really the Malay Archipelago
remains inaccurate or an insult from the mouths
who parrot the Genoese ventriloquist
who ordered hands empty of gold to be severed
who discovered the triangle for trafficking slaves
who declared this ancient world "new" and his and Spain's.
Penelope clarifies:
The people living here first   indigenous to the Americas
recount from their primal genesis to family clans that multiplied
and for generations and generations sustained
loyal to the lushness
like to deities of corn and rain.

When they named   they described what they saw
told a story   showed respect to greater powers
like with the Mayan-Carib words "Amac Ric" meaning strong
    life force.
Sometimes a name gave thanks to the land they lived on.
David says they used to live where we live now.
Lowering her voice to signal a new domestic law
Penelope speaks slowly to David her son.
We will learn names of indigenous peoples one by one
like the Inuit in the north
the Makah   the Quinault   the Yakima
the Blackfoot   the Cherokee
including the Tainos and Arawaks and Caribs
who discovered Columbus exploring the clear coast
looking to snatch gold from their necks.
David interjects he sounds like a mugger.
Penelope takes a breath and resumes.
We will study many cultures from the Maya to the Mapuche.
David says that means I got to learn thousands and thousands
    of names.

—*Zoë Anglesey*

Alaska's King Island Inupiat Dancers and Singers, photo by Marvin Inouye

CONTENTS

This book grew out of a landmark conference that took place in Los Angeles in 1990, but it was foreshadowed by an event the year before. In June 1989, the Dance Critics Association held its annual conference in San Francisco, the first time in its then fifteen-year history that the organization had met outside New York. This may not seem such a radical act. Yet for those of us living on the West Coast, it represented a significant tilt: toward the "regions" and away from New York. One of the keynote speakers for that San Francisco event, the accomplished (and controversial) director Peter Sellars, delivered a meditation on the "new cultural interface" in America, characterized by the convergence of Asian, Latin American, and African cultures. He then introduced his ambitious plans for the 1990 Los Angeles Festival, a citywide affair focusing on the arts and cultures of the Pacific. His pitch was charismatic, the buzz immediate: Why not hold the next conference in Los Angeles?

The choice of the City of Angels as the site of the organization's 1990 conference was felicitous. An international organization devoted to improving the quality of writing on dance, the Dance Critics Association boasts a long history of first-rate conferences, on subjects ranging from Marius Petipa's ballet *The Sleeping Beauty* to the concept of "text" in contemporary dance. Never before 1990, however, had DCA devoted an entire conference to the subject of non-Western, or "non-Euro-American," forms.

The time, it seemed, was right for this new focus. Sellars' event, with its concentration on dance genres seldom seen or evaluated on American soil, generated interest among even those critics openly biased toward ballet and modern dance.

Among the performers were Javanese dancers representing the Court of Yogyakarta in Java, Indonesia; Australian aboriginals from remote Mornington Island; Native Americans from the Jemez Pueblo in New Mexico. The opening ceremonies at Angel's Gate—a breathtakingly beautiful site overlooking the Pacific Ocean—included representatives from Tonga, the Ikooc people of southern Mexico, Chindo Shamans from Korea, Hālau O'Kakuhi from Hawai'i's Big Island, and the Waiwhetu Maori Cultural Group from New Zealand, among others.

But the appeal of the Los Angeles Festival went beyond its programming. It was in 1990, after all, that the debate over political correctness was reaching its climax. "Multiculturalism" was the word on everyone's lips. And just two years later, America would be celebrating (or lamenting) the five hundredth anniversary of Columbus' voyage, viewed now with ambivalence as the defining event in American history.

And so it was that from August 31 to September 3, 1990, "Looking Out" virtually exploded on the campus of California State University, Los Angeles. (The conference was enhanced by an accompanying "Multicultural Scholarship Program," an encouragement to people of color to enter the field of dance writing.) Nearly three hundred critics, scholars, artists, and audience members were in attendance: arguing, debating, and Looking Out at dances from around the world.

With noteworthy exceptions, all of the entries in this book found their genesis at the Los Angeles conference as speeches, conversations, or interviews. (Fresh contributions include articles by Joan Acocella, Peter Nabokov, Lewis Segal, and more than a dozen critics who share here their reviews of Javanese *Bedhaya*.) This book is not, however, a standard conference transcript, but rather an anthology of writings on dance that has substantially grown, changed, and deepened since 1990.

All the authors have refined their contributions, incorporating ideas developed over the subsequent years. It is my hope, and the hope of the Dance Critics Association, that the debate about dance criticism of forms from around the world has been furthered by the care and depth of thinking with which the authors have reconsidered their work.

The book's coeditors have been particularly instrumental in seeing this collection through to completion. Lewis Segal of the *Los Angeles Times* and Elizabeth Zimmer, now of the *Village Voice*, served as enthusiastic partners with me in planning the 1990 conference, and they have continued as effective collaborators throughout the shaping of this book. Patrice Koelsch, the former executive director of the Center for Arts Criticism in St. Paul, Minnesota, joined our team soon after the conference, adding a healthy perspective on the role of criticism in other artistic genres. I am grateful to all three for their skill and perseverance.

Also essential in getting this project off the ground were members of an advisory committee of scholars and critics who provided start-up advice. I thank Brenda Dixon Gottschild, Deborah Jowitt, Alan M. Kriegsman, Chiori Santiago, Gus Solomons jr, and Ricardo D. Trimillos for helping in this capacity. Stephen Steinberg served as coordinator of the book project until his death from complications of AIDS in 1991. He remains an inspiration to us, especially through the example of his fine dance monographs published by the San Francisco Performing Arts Library and Museum.

In addition to the authors and photographers, whose ideas and keen sensibilities have brought this book to life, several "backstage" contributors deserve special acknowledgment: Wendell Ricketts, whose skill in working with words has won my deep respect yet again; Rachel Kaplan, a first-rate transcriber and significant source of encouragement; Richard Carlin, who served as our editor and sympathetic liaison at Schirmer Books; and the production team of Cal Anderson and Jeffrey Brandenburg, two of the best book design professionals in the business.

Others who have assisted in ways both large and small are Don Bondi, Lori Brungard, Peter Carley, Arline Chambers, Tim Choy, Rachel Cooper, Susan Chung, Doris Diether, Bruce Fleming, Norman Frisch, Daniel Goldstein, Judith Green, Clifford Harper, Linda Kostalik, Robert McEwen, Judy Mitoma, Gay Morris, Nita Little Nelson, Barbara Palfy, Nicole Plett, Sarah Pollock, Renée Renouf, Janice Ross, Peter Sellars, Joanne Shwed, Gordy Slack, Becky Stone, Harriet Swift, the late Allen Wallace, and Eric Weissler of the firm of Armstrong Hirsch Jackoway Tyerman & Wertheimer. Our thanks to them.

Significantly, this book could not have come into being without the generous financial support of the Jerome Foundation and Mervyn's, two visionary funders who recognized the catalytic effect this discussion could have on the field of dance criticism and dance in general. They are the major underwriters of this publication. Support for the 1990 conference itself was provided by the California Arts Council; the California Council for the Humanities, a state program of the National Endowment for the Humanities; the City of Los Angeles Cultural Affairs Department; The James Irvine Foundation; the Los Angeles Times; Philip Morris Companies Inc.; Lloyd E. Rigler and Lawrence E. Deutsch of Los Angeles; The Rockefeller Foundation; and the Zellerbach Family Fund.

David Gere
Editor

LOOKING OUT

INTRODUCTION

David Gere

Reading this book is a bit like peering into the eye of a storm. Swirling about are key words emblazoned on spinning placards: *cultural equity, colonialism, artistic hegemony, authenticity, identity, ethnic dance, world dance,* and, of course, the big three—*multiculturalism, political correctness,* and the mysterious-sounding *Other.* The temptation, of course, is to dismiss these as buzzwords. And yet, given the stunning pervasiveness of their use in the dance world of the 1990s, to do so would be akin to burying our heads in the sand. In fact, the purpose of this book—which started as a conference and has turned into an anthology—is to pull our heads *out* of the sand, to engage fiercely in the most crucial debates of our time.

Here, then, is an overview of the issues at hand.

SHIFTING THE CANON

Even as universities have placed certain books at the core of their curriculum, the field of dance criticism—and, it could be argued, the dance field in general—has fixed on a relatively rigid canon of dances for study and reflection. To be an "insider," one is required to know these dances, to have seen them (even on video), or to have read about them. Significantly for the dance field, this canon forms the basis of a loosely shared aesthetic system referred to by critics when making judgments about performance and choreography.

◄ *A young dancer in Sanur, Bali, photo © Bonnie Kamin*

The vast majority of works in the American version of the canon represents ballet or modern dance, from *Giselle* on the ballet side to Martha Graham's *Appalachian Spring* and Alvin Ailey's *Revelations* on the modern. Nearly all are Euro-American in origin. You might call them the Great Dances of the Western World.

It has been argued, especially by a growing coalition of underrepresented artists, that the canon ought to be broadened to include a wider range of dance forms and choreography. New cultures, new artists, new approaches to the avant-garde, and a large dollop of the non-Western—these are the rallying cries of the so-called multiculturalists. And the West Coast multiculturalists, as Stanford professor Renato Rosaldo suggests, cry out with a particular urgency:

> California is particularly vulnerable to the effects of global interdependence, decolonization, and the decline of North American hegemony. The implosion of the Third World into the First has perhaps reached a more advanced stage here. In grades K to 12, for example, California schools now have a majority of minority students. Even conservative demographers estimate that, within twenty years, the state's population will be forty percent of Mexican ancestry, twenty percent other non-white, and forty percent white.[1]

Thus, as Bruce Fleming suggests in this volume's title essay, what we are experiencing now in dance—especially in the West—is fully comparable to the "displacement of the Ptolemaic earth-centered paradigm of the universe by the Galilean insistence that the earth moved around the sun." The Euro-American dances that had been the central reference points

---

1. "Others of Invention: Ethnicity and its Discontents," *Village Voice Literary Supplement* (February 1990), 27–28.

for the field have been forced to shift, to make room for dances originating in other parts of the world.

PREJUDICE

But as the canon shifts, so do interpretations of it. Some writers and scholars—notably Brenda Dixon Gottschild—have suggested that American dance is a product of African influences as well as European. So why has the deep vein of Africanist aesthetics been systematically ignored or denied? In her essay in this volume, Gottschild cites Elvis Presley's imitation of African-American musical styles as the best-known example of Africanist influence going unacknowledged and unrewarded in America. In dance, she looks closely at the ballets of George Balanchine, proposing that Africanisms are key elements of Balanchine's "American" style.

Allegra Fuller Snyder, meanwhile, points her lens at the depiction of non-Western dance in Hollywood films, identifying the cluster of "sinister symbols"—from snakes to malevolent "voodoo" rituals—that Hollywood has used to define the realm of the "primitive." Hollywood dance depictions will change, Snyder contends, only when cultural envoys "have the right to speak out and represent themselves in film and video."

Other writers in this volume are concerned with racism in the dance community as a whole. Jawole Willa Jo Zollar sees it as a "twisted growing thing" that has taken root in the soil of American dance, tainting the entire field. Joan Acocella, meanwhile, challenges the scope of Zollar's definition, arguing that it smears everyone impartially.

Throughout, the writers in this volume express their discomfort with what Fleming derides as the "sanctimonious air" of multicultural partisans and what Deborah Jowitt acknowledges as the insensitivity of some writers to the aesthetics and context of unfamiliar dance forms. A pair of rhetorical questions defines the extremes: Is the shift in the canon and its interpretation being legislated by angry mobs? Or is it a thoughtful response to new information and self-reflection?

TERMINOLOGY AND HIERARCHIES

Then, of course, there is the question of terminology. On its face, the word "multiculturalism" is an all-inclusive term that means, literally, "many cultures." In common practice, however, it refers exclusively to people of color, to gays and lesbians, to any group that does not belong to the straight white majority.

A similar semantic problem follows the terms "ethnic dance" and "world dance." In a twenty-five-year-old essay cited frequently in this book, anthropologist Joann Kealiinohomoku argued definitively for the notion that all dances are ethnic, including classical ballet. But when the term "ethnic dance" became contaminated as a (pejorative) label for non-Western dance, some theorists and writers switched to "world dance." It didn't work. Not only did "world dance" continue as a label for the non-Western, but the new term implied that Euro-Americans were not part of the world. Current newspaper listings often classify dance as "ballet," "modern," and "ethnic." So do educational institutions and funders. Kealiinohomoku, in a recent essay (not included in this volume), has suggested retiring the terms "ethnic dance" and "world dance" altogether, seeking instead to label dance forms with their own genre names, as, for instance, Bharata Natyam or flamenco or ballet.[2]

The history of the term "ethnic dance" also reflects a skirmish over the establishment and maintenance of hierarchies, of unwritten lists that value certain forms of dance over certain others. In dance criticism, for instance, the practice of categorizing dance as ballet, modern, or ethnic is commonly reflected in the number of inches of copy devoted to each

---

2. "Angst Over Ethnic Dance," *Cross-Cultural Dance Resources Newsletter* (Summer 1990), 1–2, 5–6.

classification. Most daily newspapers consider the dance season over when the local ballet company finishes its ten weeks, and, as any publicist knows, there is nothing tougher than getting critics to attend a so-called "ethnic" performance. No wonder the multiculturalists argue for the destruction of hierarchies, for the value-free acceptance of all dance forms, for equal treatment in everything from funding to criticism.

And yet, on the reverse side, *New York Times* music critic Edward Rothstein, writing in *The New Republic*, argues that multicultural partisans are mistaken when they argue that "no judgment can be made between musics on the basis of intrinsic value because there is no hierarchy in the arts."[3] This principle, he contends, "condescends to the very cultures for which it demands 'equity,' because it refuses even their own distinctions." In other words, if the citizens of India consider concert performances of Carnatic music of higher intrinsic value than spontaneous renditions of religious *bhajans*, who are we to ignore the hierarchy of their culture? Similarly, if more Americans attend performances of ballet than of, say, Appalachian clogging, or if they place it in an elevated position, doesn't that make ballet preeminent? The concept of hierarchy is further complicated, of course, in America's multicultural society, where we are not only comparing the Indian to the Indian and the Euro-American to the Euro-American, but the Indian to the Euro-American to the African-American to the Latino. If acceptable hierarchies are to arise in America, they must apply across cultures.

In this volume, the controversy is reflected indirectly in Joan Acocella's argument for the importance of artistic "preferences." Acocella celebrates her native response to Aristotelian form, but, as an American who has imbibed the whole range of American influences, she also feels a special affinity for

---

3. "Roll Over Beethoven: The New Musical Correctness and its Mistakes," *The New Republic* (4 February 1991), 29–34.

African dancing, as illustrated by her encounter with the Milwaukee troupe Ko-Thi. Meanwhile, Marcia B. Siegel's emphasis (in the same discussion) on description as opposed to evaluation in her criticism aligns her closely with the hierarchy-breaking multiculturalists. "I try not to be judgmental," she says, striving instead for the dancing to reveal itself on its own terms.

On a related front, the framing essays by Fleming and Siegel limn a debate over the motivations for embracing dances from outside the canon. Does the proposed expansion of the canon stem from the desire for a new "exoticism" (fresh stimulation for jaded palates) or does it indicate a respectable search for artistic revitalization?

CRITICISM AND ETHNOGRAPHY

Another recurring theme concerns the role of the critic versus that of the ethnographer, of the judge who evaluates works within the culture (from the canon) versus the anthropologist working to describe and make sense of artifacts or dances created by the cultural Other (from outside the canon). "As critics we can't be bootstrap ethnologists," writes Deborah Jowitt. "Assuming such a stance only burdens our prose and alienates our readers and, anyway, the few real ethnologists would snort at what we said because we couldn't possibly come up to snuff in a short time." And yet, according to ethnomusicologist Ricardo D. Trimillos, critics are already functioning in contemporary American society as de facto cross-cultural commentators. If Trimillos is right, do critics have any choice but to dip into ethnographic territory?

As Sally Banes pointed out in her keynote address to the 1989 Dance Critics Association conference, there are clear differences between the critic and the ethnographer, in terms of locale, research method, and the presence or absence of evaluation in the final written product.[4] But these differences have grown increasingly fuzzy since the 1960s, when dance criticism began to address nontheatrical dance experiences—such as vernacular and folk dances, or nondance movement events such as figure skating or parades—and ethnographers, facing a crisis of confidence, began to question the authority of the Western observer. Banes finds a fusion of the two roles impossible because of the disjuncture in their approach to the collection of information. "Who wants to coauthor their review with the choreographer?" she asks, contrasting the critic's predilection for independent analysis with the ethnographer's for dialogic editing. And yet, with both fields dabbling in the realm of daily life and increasingly underplaying authority and evaluation, there seems to be a vast gray area between the two that screams out for the possibility of a new fusion or, at the very least, of collegial working relationships between practitioners of the two modes.

Surely the experience of crossing back and forth between the realms of ethnography and criticism will become more common as the multicultural era progresses. The Dance Critics Association has already undertaken an initiative to attract more writers of color into the field, in part to encourage criticism by knowledgeable insiders. Ethnographers are a major target group. And, as an increasing number of established critics lead double lives in academia and journalism—as Banes, Jowitt, Siegel, Gay Morris, and Janice Ross, to name only a few, have done already—the ability to share information with ethnographers within the walls of the academy will be greatly facilitated. Perhaps the two fields are not so different after all.

---

4. "Criticism as Ethnography," reprinted in Sally Banes, *Writing Dancing in the Age of Postmodernism* (Hanover and London: Wesleyan University Press/University Press of New England, 1994), pp. 16–24.

The Aesthetics of Transfer

It would be useful to set both critics and ethnographers to work on the central project of American multiculturalism at the end of the century: divining what could be called "the aesthetics of transfer," from nonproscenium environments to the proscenium stage, and from international locales to America. As more and more dance forms find their way to America via widening circles of immigration and international exchange, dance critics are being called upon to expand their ability to describe, interpret, and evaluate forms of dance with which they have no inherent cultural affinity. Without developing the means for evaluation, dance critics are in danger of writing what Acocella calls "genteel" or "UNICEF" reviews, reviews that talk about pretty costumes but avoid the analytical processes that are the essence of criticism.

Evaluation, however, involves more than proclaiming what is good and what is bad about a particular dance or dance company. It requires a sensitive consideration of such issues as authenticity and cultural entitlement—discussed at length here by Trimillos—and it also involves a hard look at the process by which the choreographer (or, just as likely, the presenter) adapts a particular dance or dance form for the proscenium stage, as Lewis Segal outlines in his prescient essay. The contributors to "Geography of the Sacred" reveal that the resonance of a particular place can prove key. How can that resonance be recaptured in a new setting?

Equally important, from an aesthetic standpoint, is the development of a new critical framework to deal with issues of cross-cultural fusion, which Guillermo Gómez-Peña describes in a performance text as the "vernacular postmodern sensibility."

Mark Morris' eclectic movement vocabulary, for instance, is based in part upon his early experiences in a Balkan folk dance group and incorporates rhythms and imagery drawn from his knowledge of Spanish dance, Kathak, and ballet. Is

Morris' approach a form of cultural imperialism, as Siegel suggests in her "On Multiculturality" essay? Or is it the new multicultural aesthetic in action? Are the aesthetics of dances from around the world to be protected as if they were nuclear material, requiring careful regulation (by critics? ethnographers?) lest they be misused? Or is the world of dance open for free exchange?

PLUNGING IN

This book is full of questions, but it is also packed with answers in the form of firsthand accounts by dance writers of their experience in writing about dance from around the world. More than a dozen points of view are evident in the section of reviews led off by Alastair Macaulay's overnight piece on Javanese *Bedhaya*. Still other approaches are evaluated by June Vail in her study of articles on the Indian dancers Indrani and Sukanya. Similarly practical is a rich discussion on "Coming to Grips with the 'Other,'" featuring three of the country's most esteemed dance critics—Jowitt, Acocella, and Siegel.

Lest the project of writing about dance in a multicultural world become completely daunting, it might be heartening to recall other periods in recent American dance history when seismic shifts took place. When modern dance came into full flower in the 1930s, many critics resisted (John Martin was a formidable exception). In the 1960s, a new generation of critics cringed when asked to cover dance out-of-doors or in cramped loft spaces (Jill Johnston broke that mold).

So here we are in the 1990s, trying to make sense of the next major dance phenomenon of the century, resisting again, perhaps, but with a growing sense of excitement at the possibilities ahead. One day this may be known as the era when American dance embarked on its most important project: defining and refining the art of Looking Out.

LOOKING OUT

Bruce Fleming

"World dance": the term itself is new, its adoption for general use the sign of an alteration in sensibility that merits consideration. For in this term are hidden presuppositions and assumptions which, if they are not exactly false, should at least be brought to light so that they can be considered on their own merits. And it may very well be that their merit is not quite as great as it initially seemed.

"World dance" as a term to refer to non-Western dance replaces, for the culturally sensitized, the semipejorative "ethnic dance" that is still common currency in some circles. The labeling of anything non-Western as "ethnic" is clearly a value judgment, underlining the primacy of one particular cultural matrix: it implies that there is, on the one hand, standard dance; outside of this there is merely folklore.

Indeed, the insistence that the standards of white people of northern European stock not be used as a measure of value for all artistic products is heard and seen nowadays in virtually all American professional organizations and journals, from the meetings of the Modern Language Association to *College Art*, the magazine of the American College Art Association.

In recognition of this essay, Fleming was named the 1990 Dance Critics Association Fellow. Some of the ideas herein are further developed in Fleming's "The Voice in My Ear: Ennosuke's Kabuki," *New Dance Review* 4:3 (1992), 17–20; and in his *Caging the Lion: Cross-Cultural Fictions* (New York: Peter Lang, 1993).

◀ *Ichikawa Ennosuke III as the Demon in "Kurozuka," photo © Jack Vartoogian*

This itself is part of a yet larger cultural agon. Universities debate the inclusion or exclusion of literary works by non-white, nonstraight males into the canon; museum directors clash with ethnographers on the most suitable way to display the art objects of Africa and Oceania—should the formal qualities of the works be emphasized by showing them on pedestals in a museum with white walls, or are they comprehensible only in the larger and more specific context of the society which produced them?

My first point, therefore, is that the effort within the field of dance criticism to "look out" is not an isolated blip on a screen. It is part of a much larger wave; this book is as much following a trend as making one. So, too, was Peter Sellars as much a trend-follower as a trend-setter in deciding to devote the 1990 Los Angeles Festival to the arts of Pacific cultures—which means largely non-Western ones. Sellars' curatorial emphasis was yet another example of the alteration of sensibility that American sociologists have expressed as the abandonment of the paradigm of the "melting pot" for our society and the adoption of one sometimes called the "beef stew": lots of chunks, rather than one smooth consistency in the mixture.

This cultural trend is earthshaking in its implications for America. I do not think it is too much to compare it to the displacement of the Ptolemaic earth-centered paradigm of the universe by the Galilean insistence that the earth moved around the sun: like the earth and man upon it, Caucasians of western European origin are no longer the center of the universe; instead "Euro-Americans" must acknowledge that there are other planets of equal value, all of which (it may be) circle round a single source of artistic inspiration.

American dance critics have, it seems, been taught for too long that women deforming their feet in strange hard-tipped shoes in order to stand, of all things, on their toes, and dancers of both sexes opening feet and hips in ways that God never intended them to do, is (in the words of Keats' urn) all ye know on earth, and all ye need to know. It is—and here I am stating a personal conviction as well as summarizing an overall trend—clearly time to acknowledge the fact that there is indeed more in heaven and on earth than was dreamt of in our philosophy of dance, as anyone attending a performance in a dance form strange to him or her will attest. Looking out (which is to say, looking outwards), acknowledging our own limitations and contingency: this is clearly a good thing, a humble thing, indeed one might say a godly thing, helping to free us as it does of the sin of pride.

And yet for all of the virtuous, even self-congratulatory feelings this openness to cultures other than our own may produce, it is not easy to know how to put this openness into practice. Indeed, there are problems with the result even if we are able to do so. And it is to these problems that I wish to turn now, in order to make what is the second main point of this paper.

We may take for granted the point of the ethnographers: that all art forms spring from a particular culture. (In her essay "An Anthropologist Looks at Ballet as a Form of Ethnic Dance," Joann Kealiinohomoku outlines the cultural givens undergirding the classical ballet—as if it were a surprise to hear that it possesses such.[1] Of course the classical ballet presupposes cultural givens; of course the only reason we do not see this is that we take them for granted.) The difference between the products of Western culture and those of non-Western cultures is not that they are specific to their cultures while ours are somehow universally comprehensible, transcending the specificities of culture. Yet the fact remains that there is a fundamental difference for the perceiver between a work

---

1. Impulse (1969–1970), 24–33; reprinted in Roger Copeland and Marshall Cohen, eds., What is Dance? (New York: Oxford University Press, 1983), pp. 533–549.

whose cultural underpinnings he or she can take for granted and a work where these are totally strange. And it is in the latter situation that we Euro-Americans find ourselves when we sit at concerts of "world dance."

As an example of this fundamental difference between works of one's own culture and works of other cultures for the perceiver, I offer an experience I had in 1990 at a performance of a Japanese kabuki troupe led by the celebrated actor Ennosuke, which (as a result) was billed as *Ennosuke's Kabuki* and presented at the Metropolitan Opera House and the John F. Kennedy Center. The peculiarity of this performance was the fact that in the hallway beforehand viewers were exhorted to rent, for five dollars, a headset that was advertised as "absolutely essential" to the understanding of the performance. Mine came with the press kit, or I might not have rented it. (I am one of those people who refuses to look at an art exhibition with a recorded curator talking in my ear.) The voice provided information about nearly every conceivable aspect of the performance: the term used to refer to the female impersonator actors, the plot developments, the meaning of the drum roll in the music—in short, all of the "footnotes" that the editor of a text from a long-ago era or a strange culture must provide to make that text accessible to a reader.

Because I could make this voice go away simply by pulling the plug out of my ear, I was able to switch at will from performance-with-footnotes to performance-without-footnotes. And the difference between these two radically different phenomena was that with the auditory footnotes, I "understood" what I saw, but was unable to see the performance as the end in itself that art from a culture I understand seems to be. Without the auditory footnotes, on the other hand, the performance on the stage took on to a much greater extent the visual character of a performance in ballet or modern dance, but was utterly incomprehensible, perceived the way someone ignorant of the rules of baseball would watch a Dodgers game. And yet these footnotes were not even at the base of the page, where I could look at them at my leisure— but instead (so to say) interspersed through the text, simultaneous with it, so that it was impossible to see the performance as an individual event. Instead, it became the example of a type that was being explained to me over the headset. The voice-over was both destructive, that is, and absolutely necessary.

If I were Japanese, of course, I might more readily be able to take for granted all of the things that the voice filled me in on—just as I now go to a performance of *Giselle* knowing the plot, accepting the position of turnout from the dancers, regarding the mad scene as an essential feature of the work's Romanticism, and not finding inherently foreign the notion that the dead might well be conceived of as existing in spirit form, flitting through the woods. Without such information I do not, we may say, understand *Giselle*. Without comparable information for dance from other traditions, partisans of world dance would insist, I cannot hope to understand the kabuki. And their conclusion from this is precisely that we as audience members must educate ourselves, must learn the givens and the variables in the products of other cultures, just as we learn more gradually, and almost by osmosis, similar things for our own cultures. (That the givens of classical ballet and modern dance are in fact learned is clear to me from teaching dance works from films and performances to midshipmen at the United States Naval Academy, who take for granted neither tights, toeshoes, turnout, nor tutus.)

In fact, I agree with what would certainly be the reaction of world dance partisans to such a situation as that in which I found myself at the kabuki. We cannot, in fact, fully appreciate the products of another culture until we have internalized a vast list of cultural givens that serves as the hidden part of the iceberg supporting the tip—the tip being the program that is presented to us from eight in the evening until ten-thirty. Yet now we come to the heart of the problem, which has both its practical and theoretical sides.

First of all, to the practical. It is, let me state flatly, utterly beyond the bounds of possibility to ask the average viewer to educate him- or herself before such a performance in an unfamiliar form to the point where he or she will "understand" *this* performance. Indeed, I would suggest that understanding art consists of knowing what to look for. Art is not created in a realm separate from the world; instead, artworks include some of the givens of a particular world and add to them elements that are not part of that world. Experience teaches us to situate the dividing line between that proportion of the quotidian which every artwork contains, and that which is added individually by the artist. We appreciate the artistic side of an object or an event only in contrast to that which it accepts and incorporates without change from the world. This process, of course, admits of stages, and we can understand more or less at any given time—which is to say, see more or less of what makes the artwork in question art.[2]

Even assuming that we critics learn enough about the form to stumble through a few general pointers regarding what to look for, most of us cannot do enough advance articles to impart this information—and if we could, how could we guarantee that the audience would have read them? Require them to pass a test before they enter the theater?

Well, some critics say, the answer is adequate program notes, something that has been criminally lacking in most commercially produced world dance concerts. But here again, practicality kicks us in the leg. The fact of the matter is that

---

2. For a fuller development of Fleming's ideas on this subject, see his *Essay in Post-Romantic Literary Theory: Art, Artifact, and the Innocent Eye* (Lewiston, NY: Edwin Mellen Press, 1991).

people do not usually get to the theater in time to read program notes, or are talking with their neighbors or having people climb over them. And this is what certainly impelled the promoters of *Ennosuke's Kabuki* to offer the concert head-set—an experiment that I must proclaim a resounding failure. It is too distracting, and it makes the performance into a teaching tool for the generic, rather than something to be perceived, at least consciously, as a specific performance.

The practical problems facing those who would have us "understand" world dance, therefore, are daunting. But the theoretical problem is worse. For even if we somehow acquire, as critics or as audience members, a minimal fluency in the givens of those few major non-Western art forms that we Westerners may expect to see more than once in a lifetime, the most we can get from this stumbling acquaintance is a relationship with the works of these other cultures which approaches, perhaps asymptotically, that relationship we already have with those of our own. We can get to know more quantitatively, but we do not hope to know qualitatively more.

What this means is that Euro-American viewers can become more familiar with non-Western cultures and their dances—and curiosity may well impel us to do so. But the paradoxical fact we must confront at the end of this process (a paradox which Proust articulated many decades ago in his *Remembrance of Things Past*) is that by bringing the outside inside, we render it banal—by domesticating the exotic, that is to say, we are left not with an accessible exotic, but only with the domestic. By attaining visual fluency in the dance forms of other cultures we may keep ourselves intellectually busy for decades. Yet the result can at best be merely more of what we started with in the beginning: a near-native fluency in a certain number of languages, not a fundamentally Other sort of comprehension.

And what this suggests is that there is no *moral* compulsion to engage in such a process. If we are curious, I repeat, let us do so by all means. I am curious, and I imagine most members of the critical community are curious too. But we must divest ourselves immediately of our feeling of somehow being "politically correct" or morally sensitized in our actions in a way that others are not, as if we were more tolerant, or more open, than those who would really rather watch boring ballet and mouldy modern dance.

There is an air of the sanctimonious exuded by many scholars and critics who have climbed on the "world dance" bandwagon that bothers me. For that matter, even the term bothers me, for if "world dance" is dance from Out There, what are we here at home? Other-worldly? Indeed, it may not merely be provocation to say that the greater openness to the world on which partisans of world dance pride themselves is in fact nothing but sordid appropriation, intellectual colonization under another name. What the most vocal partisans of the necessity to "understand" world dance propose is nothing but the systematic intellectual digestion of new foods, sought out precisely because they are necessary to titillate our now-jaded Western palate. Indeed, some of the more honest of the proponents of world dance have explicitly linked the growing Western interest in non-Western dance to a fading of vitality on the domestic avant-garde scene. Critics and promoters are suddenly interested in the rest of the world, that is, because the scene at home is becoming uninteresting. Yet we should remind ourselves that all this dance existed for a good long time before we decided we were interested in it. We need not congratulate ourselves for finally getting around to looking at it, and we are ill-advised to castigate others who do not currently feel the need to do so.

Indeed, we may relativize our current openness to other cultures even further, by pointing out that it is, in its turn, only the latest turn of the post-Romantic screw, the expression of a sensibility that is definitive of our Modernity. For part of the definition of Western Modernity (which, for literary history, begins perhaps with *Madame Bovary*; for dance history perhaps with Isadora Duncan and Ruth St. Denis) is our disgust with ourselves, our conviction that we are not the best of all civilizations but, indeed, probably the worst. And the flip side of this malaise with Western civilization (which we can see in writers, artists, and thinkers stretching from Rousseau through the Romantics and Freud up to our day) is the belief that Out There, people are different.

Modernist art almost takes this notion as definitive. Yet it was not the Moderns who articulated it first; this honor goes to the Romantics, who crystallized and somehow deepened a comparatively trivial contrast between the classical and modern ages that was common currency in eighteenth-century European thought. The Romantic form of this notion with which we are most familiar is Rousseau's conception of the noble savage—the idea that more elemental people with less "civilization" were somehow kinder, gentler, or at least more in touch with their feelings than the decadent Europeans. (For Marie Antoinette and her serving women who played at milkmaids at Versailles, the noble savage was as close as the peasant's cow field.) We see this malaise with city/Europe/ Caucasianness in Shelley and Wordsworth, in Schiller, in Delacroix, in Alfred de Musset—indeed, Musset thought it was the "sickness of the century."[3] And a generation later it

---

3.   The most seminal work of Rousseau for his notion of the noble savage is his *Discourse on the Origin of Inequality.* Numerous poems by Shelley, Byron, Wordsworth, and others of the English Romantics express their weariness with cities, England, and the rationalistic mind-set of the West in general. Schiller made the distinction between "naïve" and "sentimental" that is central to this discussion in *On Naïve and Sentimental Poetry.* De Musset's weariness with the world found expression most succinctly in his *Confession of a Child of the Century,* where he coined the phrase "*mal de siècle,*" what we would call existential world-weariness. Delacroix's fascination with charging steeds and languorous harem women is well documented; the Freud who seems most akin to the Romantics in this sense is the author of *Civilization and its Discontents.*

was something like this belief in a simpler, more elementary or direct world Out There that drove Gauguin to Tahiti, sent Bartók and Kodály into the villages of Hungary to record folk songs, set the German Expressionists to making sculptures that virtually mimic African ritual objects, produced the Cubism of Braque and Picasso and the fascination with the Chinese ideogram of Ezra Pound and Sergei Eisenstein.

It was also a diluted version of this that found its way into the American Indian-influenced *Primitive Mysteries* of Martha Graham, the dreamy mysticism of St. Denis' "oriental" solos, and the works that Erick Hawkins still offers today—and, of course, the third-generational form, the highly sophisticated cross-cultural works of artists like Meredith Monk and Kei Takei, with dozens of other artists—including Arthur Mitchell and Billy Wilson, Jerome Robbins, and even George Balanchine himself—drawing on "exotic" sources as the inspiration for particular works.

Yet these Moderns were more honest about their appropriations than we now tend to be. Back then, they could acknowledge that they frankly sought the Exotic—which is to say, the Other that was meant to stay Other, even when it was displayed on the stages and museums of the appropriating culture. The Romantics and the Moderns were frankly pillagers—bringing back fragments of other worlds Out There and setting them up in museums, putting them on their canvases or in their books as exotic backgrounds, translating them into the "ethnic" divertissements of Moorish or Spanish or Chinese dances in full-length ballets, or as ends in themselves in the style of St. Denis. Nowadays we pat ourselves on the back by saying that we no longer pillage. Instead we try to comprehend, to understand other cultures on their own terms. The exotic is out, explanation is in.

One example of this is seen in the fact that African art was initially displayed in the West in ethnographic museums; then for a time it was considered evidence of cultural sensitivity to accord it the status of our own art objects—at which point it moved to Plexiglas stands under spotlights before white walls. Now the trend is to bring it back into the ethnographic museum, to insist that it is part of a larger context, that it is not merely an object of disinterested contemplation. Yet under these circumstances such objects, I find, tend to fade into the light of common day, becoming just as comprehensible, and banal, as our own designer lamps and stainless steel toasters.

I believe that it is still an interest in a world outside we take to be alluringly Other that drives our interest in world dance, as it is in things like African sculptures: they are something different. (We are the children of our parents, the Modernists, after all.) Yet nowadays we do not frequently acknowledge that this is so. And the result is that world dance is now caught somewhere between the second and third of the stages I have outlined with respect to African art objects. In some places it is progress to get it on the stage of the major culture palace; in others it is progress to get it off these stages and into the classroom or at least a local ethnic society.

Though we are fueled by our desire for the transgression of borders into a fascinating Other world that we inherited from the Romantics and Modernists, we lack the honesty nowadays to acknowledge that this is so. And the problems this produces are the same in the case of world dance as in that of the display of African masks. Do we take out of context, and risk incomprehension, or do we fill in the context—assuming we can find a way to do so without totally destroying the performance as performance—and bring ourselves closer to the same boredom with this art form that sent us in the first place from the forms we understand? These are the problems of the in-between time in which we currently find ourselves with respect to world dance. Yet it may be that this in-between time will turn out to have been the most exciting.

MORE THAN ART

Ricardo D. Trimillos

We academics have a close kinship with arts critics, members of the Fourth Estate. To begin, we are both *post-facto* to the creative event. Our *raison d'être* is not to create. Rather we take a creative expression and describe, evaluate, censure, promote, or explicate it: the critic for the greater glory of a byline under a prestigious masthead (and perhaps even syndication); the academic for the rewards of tenure, promotion, and an impressively long vita. In a word, both our professions are parasitic, dependent upon the creative acts of others.

We are also alike in our methods. We observe an evanescent amalgam of movement and sound in a temporally defined space and then reduce it to the printed word—a symbol of authority and permanence in modern society. Our ability to do this empowers us, and it privileges us socially, if not economically, above the folk and third-world artists who often comprise our raw data. Thus, at even this most elemental relationship between art and art commentator, there exists a political relationship defined by economics, status, and class. Also at this most elemental relationship there exists a bond between critic and academic, for we are both arts commentators. Comfortable in the thought that we are of the same ilk and of a common mold, I assume a spirit of collective exploration. Or as we say in Hawaiian pidgin, "No shame, no ac' eh; it's jus' us."

◄   *Students at the Beijing Dance Academy, photo © Jack Vartoogian*

With that in mind, I'd like to frame the political dimensions of arts exchanges by means of a series of quotations, the first of which is by Peter Sellars, director of the 1990 Los Angeles Festival:

> There is a classic Western tradition of the artist as an exile in his own *country* [my emphasis] standing apart from the society in a gesture of superiority and refusal. . . . The need is for art that feels its place at the center of the community, the place it occupies in most traditional *societies* [my emphasis] around the globe, societies in which the working definitions of "traditional" and "contemporary" are not mutually exclusive.[1]

Sellars' comment illustrates the classic paradigm of "the self vs. the other" or "us vs. them," a formulation revealing a political mindset that certainly reflects our American biases. In the description of the classic Western tradition, that is, the "us," he uses the term "country," a political construct, and uses the singular form of the noun. In the description of "them," however, he uses the term "societies," a social construct, and uses the plural form of the noun. Further, Sellars implies that our situation is not ideal and in need of change while that of the undefined "other" is positive and to be emulated. Thus the statement provides us with the unlikely comparison of a single apple with an undifferentiated group of oranges, in which the apple is found wanting. The "us" is singular and unique; the "other" is manifold and undifferentiated. The political formulation is one of comparison and judgment.

A second quotation is by Lu Yi-sheng, principal of the Beijing Dance Academy, whom I had the opportunity to meet at the fifth Hong Kong International Dance Conference in August 1990:

---

1. Peter Sellars, "Welcome," 1990 *Los Angeles Festival Program Book*, p. 15.

> The Beijing Dance Academy is known as "the cradle of dancers." . . . The achievement in dance performance not only brings our ballet standard up to international recognition, but also *our folk dances* [my emphasis], which are enjoyed by audiences all over the world. . . . The Academy has already established exchange agreements with the Moscow Dance School, The Royal Academy of Dance, the Singapore Nanyang Institute of the Arts, and the Hong Kong Academy for Performing Arts.[2]

Lu's statement contains points germane to our topic. He measures his institution's accomplishments in ballet (a non-Chinese form) against "international" recognition, the authority for that recognition stemming from the very same classic Western tradition about which Sellars has reservations. The Chinese obsession with ballet is itself remarkable, for it signals tacit acceptance of Western cultural imperialism, a condition that China, after 1949, officially rejected.

In the same sentence, Lu refers to "our own folk dances"; his very formulation is politically problematic. It raises the question, whose dances are they? The majority of dances so labeled are attributed to minority groups in China, including the Yao, Dai, Tibetans, and Koreans. Conservatory presentations of these minority dances as choreographed and performed by Han Chinese are disturbingly inauthentic, suffering from terminal cuteness. Protests from carriers of these traditions are ignored, the most benign of possible reactions to criticism. This situation raises issues of cultural entitlement, ownership, and exploitation—all concerns of politics.

The final quote is from John-Mario Sevilla, a former student of mine who is now a professional dancer with the modern

---

2. Lu Yi-sheng, "Beijing Dance Academy," *International Festival of Dance Academies 1990 Program Book*, p. 23.

dance group Pilobolus. In a letter, he describes the 1990 American Dance Festival (ADF) in Durham, North Carolina:

> The opening night party [was] ... part of this cultural dance exchange that Charlie and Stephanie Reinhart [directors and founders of ADF] are spearheading. Did you hear that Charlie's starting "American Dance Festivals" in China, Japan, Korea, India and who knows where else[?] Is this what you'd call cultural *colonialism* and artistic *hegemony* [my emphases] in action?[3]

I find it remarkable that a performing artist would volunteer a political analysis. It is not that I regard dancers as politically naïve, often quite the contrary. Rather it is notable that the political ramifications of exchange constitute his initial comment. Although he probably intended the term "colonialism" in a lighthearted manner, its technical definition is in fact revealing. Colonialism, as defined by *Webster's New World Dictionary*, is "the system in which a country maintains foreign colonies for ... exploitation." Do Western dance institutions indeed colonize for artistic exploitation? Do we need to generate foreign employment opportunities for the choreographers and teachers we train? Do we need a larger, more international pool of performers and choreographers to draw upon in our quest for the best? These questions apply to more than the dance world.

The term "artistic hegemony" is equally provocative. As a society do we seek to dominate artistic expression? Do we impose our standards of dance and dance presentation on others through our media, through our scholars, our exchange teachers, and, yes, through our dance critics? If we accept both colonialism and hegemony as political concepts, it appears that we in the West may be seeking through artistic means a

---

3.   Personal communication with John-Mario Sevilla, 22 July 1990.

measure of international success, an accomplishment that at the moment seems to be eluding us militarily.

The foregoing statements from an arts purveyor, an educator, and a performer, respectively, only begin to suggest the intertwining complexities of the arts and politics. Now I would like to add three different personal perspectives, each deriving from a constituency with which I am actively involved, each with its own aesthetic, social, and political consequences.

AS THE PERFORMER

THE ONE-NIGHT STAND, OR TWO HOURS TO MAKE AN IMPRESSION

I have been a performer since age five. My initial experience was, appropriately enough, as a dancer with a Filipino group in San Jose, California. The group sought to communicate the rich cultural heritage of the Philippines to the general community. It was also a means for immigrant Filipinos to provide positive identity reinforcement for their American-born offspring. Such reinforcement was necessary for survival within a mainstream culture that stereotyped Filipinos as houseboys, stoop laborers, fast with white women, and even faster with knives.

My current performance involvement, for some twenty years, has been the Japanese koto, presenting concerts on the United States mainland and in Europe.

The performer involved in cross-cultural presentation, usually presenting his culture's art to a foreign audience, has the responsibility not only to provide an artistic experience for that audience but also to provide a window on his culture for them.

Let us take a not-so-hypothetical koto concert in Kenosha, Wisconsin, as illustration. The koto artist is faced with a dilemma. He has a maximum of two hours both to create a satisfying aesthetic experience and to represent a culture. It is one of the few opportunities for this community to hear live Japanese music. The audience, interested and open to new aesthetic experiences, has no background in koto music. In contrast, a Kenosha audience viewing I *Pagliacci* could be familiar with opera through recordings and the Metropolitan Opera broadcasts.

What kind of a koto program will best reach this audience? The performer makes adjustments based on his understanding (or misunderstanding) of his audience. For example, he guesses that none of them will understand Japanese; he has heard that Americans find Japanese singing strange and sometimes laugh at it. So he decides to omit any works with song; the entire program consists of instrumental pieces, both traditional and modern. Thus his program represents only half the koto repertory.

A second decision attempts to accommodate the musical background of his audience. Most people will be familiar with the Western tuning system. However, the traditional Japanese tuning uses half-steps slightly smaller than the tempered, Western half-step. Western listeners (including critics) may hear these intervals as being "flat," "out of tune," or "between the cracks." Since the koto is capable of infinite gradations of tuning, why not make the half-steps closer to Western ones? Unfortunately, this adjustment eliminates the aesthetic tension created by the smaller traditional intervals. In the 1960s, a similar adjustment to audience background prompted female dancers of the Ballet du Senegal to wear tops; exposed breasts might have offended some American audiences.

Finally, the artist wants to go the extra mile in cultural exchange—as a gesture of goodwill he programs a koto arrangement of Stephen Foster's "Old Black Joe." The inclusion of a plantation song in a classical concert is unusual, but to present "Old Black Joe" in post–civil rights America is provocative. With the recent memory of Japanese-made Black Sambo dolls and unfortunate comments by Japanese officials about African Americans, this attempt at goodwill might very well have the opposite result. A similar desire for rapprochement prompts a Chinese folk dance troupe to introduce a segment of breakdancing and moonwalking in their performance, to which the concert-oriented, foreign audience reacts negatively. Both are instances of cross-cultural misunderstanding further compounded.

What are the constraints for the artist in a foreign setting? As mentioned, he sees his mission as not only aesthetic but as cultural and educational. He wants his performance to be met with success, even if the criteria for success abroad may differ from traditional ones.

For Javanese *Wayang Wong* dance theater, such constraints reduce a five-hour performance to two hours, supposedly without losing any of its essence—an impossible task. In Beijing Opera, arias are either cut or eliminated (remember the possibility of foreign laughter at unfamiliar vocalization) in favor of acrobatics and visual humor. For programs of ancient hula, groups introduce changing floor formations, levels, and facings to hold the attention of a mainland American audience. The aesthetic sense of these viewers may not include the ritual meanings and the poetic imagery implicit in *hula pahu*, the sacred drum dances of ancient Hawai'i.

The visiting artist is concerned about the immediate effect of a specific performance upon a specific audience—his one-night stand. If he does not please them, they may have no interest in attending future concerts representing his culture. The important question for the performer then becomes, how can he present a performance that garners the applause of a foreign audience and yet does not do too much damage to the integrity of the tradition? The choice may work—the physical humor of Beijing Opera will please almost everyone. But it may also backfire—"Old Black Joe" as a naïve, harmonized koto arrangement informs the artistic standard against which the balance of the unfamiliar program is judged.

AS THE ACADEMIC

FOLKLORE OR FAKELORE, WHOSE DEFINITION?

As an ethnomusicologist, I am often consulted by American and European presenters interested in booking Asian or Pacific performing groups. Inevitably the question comes up, "But are they authentic?"

Immediately my internal computer runs a demographic check on the person inquiring. What are his or her parameters for authenticity? For some, it is equated with the exotic, mysterious, and even bizarre. A folkloric dance group in the Philippines kills a chicken onstage during the depiction of a harvest ritual. "Authentic!" pronounce the lovers of the bizarre. "Fakelore," I reply. The tribe represented is now largely Episcopalian and has not done blood sacrifices for at least two generations. Parenthetically, in this specific instance (and probably others) we academics have contributed to the fakelore. The group's choreographer based his version of the ritual upon early anthropological reports.

It is sometimes the foreign presenter's view of what is authentic that prevails. When a Papua New Guinea group performed in Europe, they were told not to wear their wristwatches, Adidas shoes, or sunglasses. These items are often worn at the traditional *singsing* in the highlands. However, the presenter felt these Western objects would make them appear less authentic to a European audience. But by insisting on such conditions, whose concept of authenticity was satisfied?

At an audition in Hawai'i, a visiting impresario was impressed with a hula dancer but did not hire her—her light skin color did not fulfill his concept of "Polynesian." She was, however, a member of one of the most distinguished native lineages of Hawaiian musicians and dancers in the state. Authenticity by physical appearance or "image" is commodified in Honolulu newspaper notices: "*Polynesian-looking dancers* [my emphasis] needed for Hawaiian show at ____ World." Again, our light-skinned artist of Hawaiian lineage need not apply; but dusky dancers with waist-length hair of Filipino, Chinese, and even Puerto Rican heritage will be hired. This represents an inverse racism that values image over artistry.

As a researcher in the field of Hawaiian performing arts, I am sometimes asked to comment upon or evaluate the "authenticity" or "traditionality" of a particular hula group. My colleague Adrienne Kaeppler of the Smithsonian Institution has already provided the categories of "traditional," "evolved traditional," and "airport art" to describe various categories of hula—all of which exist in Hawai'i and probably also in California.[4] However, when the question of authenticity is put to me (by a dancer from a competing group, for instance), the expectation is for an authoritative judgment. That puts me in a very delicate position.

With all these conditions in mind, I point out there are different kinds of authenticity. It can be authenticity of form. In hula, there is a canon of dance style and a repertoire of traditional dances which can be and are continually recreated in performance. Some groups emphasize this canon and this repertory. This kind of authenticity I would term the "historical."

However, there is another kind of authenticity—the "functional." Some Hawaiians have consciously amplified or varied some of the movements and have created new chants and hulas. They point out, and rightly so, that the hula tradition has always been immediately relevant to its society. As the society changes, so should hula. If the hula is to be authentic for Hawaiians of the 1990s, creativity and innovation are essential. Functionally speaking, hula as a museum piece is hardly authentic; it is in fact the opposite—it is artificial.

4. "Polynesian Dance as 'Airport Art,'" in Adrienne Kaeppler, Judy Van Zile, and Carl Wolz, eds., *Asian and Pacific Dance* (*Dance Research Annual*) (Congress on Research in Dance, 1977), 71–84.

A young hula master, Frank Hewett, created an "Aerobics Hula" performed to his own song composed in Hawaiian. It was danced by "authentic" Hawaiian women, that is, large women weighing between 150 and 200 pounds.[5] The performance is a double-edged political statement, challenging the "museum hula" purists and at the same time rejecting the tourist fantasy of all Hawaiian women as slim, brown, and doe-eyed with long, straight hair. Many Hawaiian women are large but very agile, and aerobics is part of the contemporary Hawaiian scene. This celebration of large female hula dancers is in part a reaffirmation of an older Hawaiian aesthetic and perhaps also an unconscious counterstatement to the Balanchinean ideal of the female dancer as svelte and androgynous. An aerobics hula is Hawai'i today; in contrast, hula about gods and goddesses whose powers no longer fully animate the cosmos somehow seem less relevant, especially today when many hula teachers and artists are devout Mormons. The same issue of authenticity confronts groups like the American Indian Dance Theatre, whose presentations raise questions among Native Americans and scholars of Native American performance because of their nontraditional staging.

Historical form or contemporary functionality—which is the more important authenticity? Is one more appropriate to the stage presentation than the other? And as contrast, if it is good theater, why does it have to be authentic at all?

AS THE MINORITY AMERICAN

CULTURAL ENTITLEMENT AND CULTURAL EXPLOITATION

I had considered myself a Filipino when I was growing up in California, doing the dances and singing the songs. At age

---

5.   This performance is included in the Rhapsody Films Video release *Kumu Hula: Keepers of a Culture*, by Mug-Shot Productions, 1989, coproduced by Vicky Takamine and Robert Mugge.

seventeen I went to the Philippines for the first time and discovered how really American I was—I could not hunker, I was too outspoken and direct, and I unconsciously recoiled every time a male cousin held my hand in public. The minority part of the appellation is also an inseparable (but not obsessive) part of my identity; it has encouraged pluralism as a preferred lifestyle and made me aware of the efficacy of equally workable alternatives. It has also made me sensitive to the issues of cultural entitlement, dilettantism, and exploitation.

Explicit among many minority performance groups is the issue of entitlement. Who has the right to present and to represent a tradition? I have witnessed pan–Native American powwows where Caucasian women replete with buckskins and eagle feathers have participated in dances. In Hawai'i the premier black gospel church choir has a *haole*, or Caucasian, drummer. Among the members of a Bavarian Schuhplättler group at a recent international dance festival was a Chinese boy who grew up in Upper Bavaria. In each case, the question raised by someone (or by numbers of individuals) has been, "What is he or she doing there?" If the question comes from an outsider, the point of "image" cited in the previous section is probably operative. However, when the question comes from a Native American, an African American, or a Bavarian, respectively, the issue is entitlement.

Entitlement in cross-cultural exchanges is still an unresolved issue for me; the 1990 controversy over the Eurasian role in the Broadway production of *Miss Saigon* is a case in point. To be absolutely true to character the actor can be neither Asian nor Caucasian—he must be of mixed blood. As Charlton Heston points out, "The door swings both ways."

There is yet another dimension to entitlement. For Filipino-Americans who do Filipino dance or for native Hawaiians who perform hula, their commitment to the art is a much more profound statement of identity than that of the *haole* who is into *danse orientale* or that of the non-Japanese koto player (like me). A Hawaiian in one of the University of Hawai'i hula classes expressed the condition of minorities and their cultural identity very poignantly. In a discussion with a Caucasian student, she said, "You don't have the same right to hula that I do. You can walk away from hula anytime you want. This year it's hula and probably next year it's Brazilian samba. But every day when I get up in the morning and look in the mirror, I'm Hawaiian—and I know I can never walk away from hula. It's my identity."

Does the outsider hula student internalize the folkways and lifestyle that are part of the hula? When the teacher is sick, does this student drop everything (including work) to look after the teacher? Does she remember (or know) to bring flowers or an offering to important hula occasions? Or is it just a dance activity? For the minority individual, her ethnic tradition is an inescapable link to a past—the door that swings both ways. She has greater access to it, and she can never entirely walk away from it.

Another troubling aspect related to entitlement is the outsider who presumes to speak for a minority culture. Unfortunately, it is frequently a majority person who co-opts that role. At a recent ethnomusicology convention in Arizona, a community mariachi made up of Anglos and Latinos performed. The narrator-violinist was a very assertive Anglo who, while explaining the cultural meanings of mariachi music, continually used the pronoun "we." Any individual with blond hair and painfully Anglo-accented Spanish should think twice before presuming to use that word, especially before an audience of ethnomusicologists. After the performance I met the leader, who is Mexican-American. He was completely bilingual, an animated raconteur, and would probably have been the better narrator. "Why didn't you do the introductions?" I asked. He smiled, shrugged, and said, "The other person really wanted to."

Is the outsider in each case simply a dilettante? Is there a commitment to the tradition as part of a culture, part of a people? And as contrast: for the outsider why does it have to be more than art? These are questions that continue to confront me as a minority person involved with minority cultures.

An even more difficult issue for me in this context is the co-optation of minority culture by majority society. In a provocative article entitled "Guatemala—Everybody's Indian When the Occasion is Right," Carol Henrickson chronicles how majority Hispanics have co-opted the *traje*, the indigenous Indian costume, as national dress.[6]

Similarly the Han Chinese majority has co-opted dances of minority groups into its national heritage, while treating the minorities as a social and economic underclass. Han choreographers present minority dances as cute, to the point of communicating superficiality. I have seen some of the original minority dances upon which these Han choreographies are based; it is clear that the Han Chinese have misunderstood or, even worse, misrepresented minority dance traditions. Distressing to me is the syllabus for minority dances developed at national dance conservatories. It promulgates and disseminates these questionable Han choreographies through a national and establishment infrastructure.

The co-optation of minority traditions by the majority is not necessarily with malice aforethought. What's troubling is an oft-encountered majority attitude that minority dances are easy or less profound. I just returned from a tour of China with a number of white American dancers and dance teachers involved principally with ballet and modern dance. For informal exchanges of performance with our Chinese hosts, some chose to show something "ethnic," including a Moroccan wedding dance and a Japanese folk dance. Why not present the modern dance or ballet of their profession? "Oh, this is just a fun

Han Chinese Ribbon Dance performed by
Aman International Folk Ensemble, courtesy Aman

occasion; ballet and modern are a bit too heavy." These people are not racists or insensitive, but they reflect a majority attitude that is unsettling to minority Americans.

I am sensitive to such issues, perhaps (by some people's reckoning) overly so. However, it is a sensitivity that is increasingly articulated as American minorities and third-world societies find their voice and their political leverage. What are the implications of these sentiments for such groups as the Aman International Folk Ensemble or El Mariachi UCLATAN de Mark Fogelquist, the memberships of which are both significantly majority American?

But now, back to dance criticism: I propose that the dance critic, by default, has become a cross-cultural arts commentator. A preliminary question might be, for whom does the critic write? However, a more central question for me is this: For whom is a review valuable? Performing artists often ignore it—"I never pay attention to reviews." The public attends in spite of it—"Oh, I went to the performance before I read the review," or, "If the critics pan it, it usually means I'll like it." The press agent only extrapolates in the interests of his three-dot syntax—"stunning ... colorful ... audience was breathless." In some cases, the content of a review seems less important than its presence as status symbol, a statement of the newspaper's cultural image.

I do not demean the value of the performance review for an American readership, but rather wish to intensify the contrast of its importance in the international arena, as cross-cultural arts commentary. In this arena the value of the review is major. Most international arts exchanges are political and economic investments, usually sponsored by governments. Reviews become the documents that "prove" that the tour is money well invested. Thus, in this international context the review and its writer take on a function beyond artistic commentary or anecdotal reportage. The reviewer becomes part of an international political process, whether willing or not. In the eyes of the performer's community, the critic is the spokesperson for the foreign audience; the review becomes the evaluation of the tradition seen abroad. In addition, it is often the only major reward the performer receives; few international tours make money for the artist.

With the rules of the game somewhat changed, homework before viewing a foreign, unfamiliar tradition is in order. The "rip-and-read" or "what-it-feels-like-to-me" approach may work with the ballet or performance art of *our* culture, but the stakes are greater for the arts of another culture.

There was a West Coast critic notorious for soliciting comments and eavesdropping on people's reactions about a performance during intermission. Much to the surprise and pique of these concertgoers, their comments or criticisms frequently appeared verbatim in a review. The consensus held that the reviewer should draw upon his own knowledge and his own ideas, that his practice of surreptitious quoting was unethical.

In the case of unfamiliar foreign traditions, I feel it is indeed ethical for the reviewer to seek out persons familiar with the tradition, including ethnomusicologists and dance ethnologists. They are usually most willing to suggest what to look for: the major style characteristics and the indigenous criteria for evaluation. It is then the prerogative of the writer to incorporate this information in the reviewing process. However, the critic who elects to comment from self-imposed ignorance or from a purely Western (and elitist) viewpoint does a disservice to the profession as well as to the visiting performer.

In closing I pose a series of questions for which there are no set answers. But the issues they represent can neither be ignored nor allowed to continue as points of ignorance.

☐ What is the responsibility of the critic to the performer and to the tradition he or she reviews?

☐ In the age of television and of language diversity in urban America, is the critic effectively reaching an optimal audience using only an English-language and print medium?

☐ What role should the reviewer's artistic criteria play in reviewing a performance of another culture?

☐ What is the responsibility of the critic in America as mediator between majority populations and minority ones?

Mutatis mutandis, these four questions apply equally to the scholar involved with performance traditions. Critic and scholar: we are sometimes the same person, we are of the same ilk, we are fellow travelers, we are bedfellows (strange or not), and we do need to work together. Clearly, we are dealing here with more than art.

Lewis Segal

Dance critics and audiences are trusting souls. When looking at repertory from the world outside mainstream Euro-American traditions, we usually accept it at face value. If something called the National Dance Company of China appears at the Los Angeles Music Center, we don't question its pedigree—until a so-called Mongolian Herdsman's Dance goes over the top, showing us nomads jeté-ing out of their yurts with pointed feet, classical turnout, and Soviet-style placement. Similarly, when Tibetan monks from the Dalai Lama's own Namgyal Monastery perform at UCLA, we draw conclusions about rituals that can last many hours, or even days, from picturesque fragments, reluctant to protest that such drastic editing inevitably despiritualizes a religious experience.

Obviously, dance created or evolving in different spatial conditions than those of the proscenium stage are routinely adapted for our theaters, as are participatory dances and those that last longer than the two to three hours we normally devote to a performance. Sometimes Western programming formats and moral values are imposed as well. All too often, this process fundamentally distorts and trivializes everything subjected to it. And because the result frequently emerges as mere diversionary spectacle, such work feeds some Westerners' already inflated notions of cultural superiority. One school of criticism orders us to concentrate on a work's movement

Portions of this essay first appeared in the *Los Angeles Times*.

◄ *Lecture-demonstration of Manipuri dance, Bombay, India, photo by Lewis Segal* values, another to research its cultural gestalt. Both approaches ignore the filter between the audience and whatever dance culture is being represented—never asking if, how, or why the idiom on view has been adulterated.

World dance audiences confront or evade this issue week by week in a typical season. Indeed, for Southern Californians, touring attractions such as American Indian Dance Theatre, *Africa Oyé*, and Ballet Folklórico Nacional de Chile provide something like a laboratory for the study of the ways choreographers and impresarios repackage world dance for export to Western stages. With only a little exaggeration, we might think of that process as a kind of neocolonialist imperative: O.K., world, fit your dances to our opera houses and our definitions of theatrical prime time; affirm Western ideals of physical beauty and serve our need for variety and virtuosity. If we don't like the result, it'll be your cultures that we deem unworthy—not the choices you make in adapting them or the conditions we impose. Our standards of comparison? Euro-American dance forms born to those conditions.

Offering what he called a "progress report" on American Indian Dance Theatre to the 1990 DCA "Looking Out" conference, artistic director Hanay Geiogamah spoke of "translating" Native American dance to the stage as a "complex challenge … that I had not really perceived." He described the task as involving decisions about "editing, grouping, music choice, costume choice, intensity in mood, build—just so many things that I took for granted."

Because he considers his restaged and shortened theater-dances different in function from their tribal sources, Geiogamah believes they have their own validity. Yet he recognizes the abuses that can occur: taking folk dance and, in his words, "tabbing it to death, because I really hate the tabbing and the string-'em-along little excerpts. That's a destructive and suffocating thing to do." As Geiogamah explained, tabbing, or radical condensing, occurs because "people will absolutely turn off from you if you do something to push them too far in this kind of ethnic performance experience." How far is too far? It depends on whom you ask.

In 1991, for instance, the women of Les Ballets Africains danced topless in Irvine but covered up in Pasadena—about forty-five miles away. Legal prohibitions? No. Call it site-specific aesthetics, a matter of local sponsors exercising the same kind of contractual option offered by Pilobolus and Bill T. Jones on recent tours. African nudity had become each presenter's choice, just as Festival of Indonesia offered two versions of its shadow-puppet performance on tour in 1990, a two-hour edition and an all-nighter. By 1993, the women of Les Ballets Africains were covered for their entire American tour because of sponsor requests. The watchword is accommodation.

In addressing the 1989 DCA *On the Edge* conference in San Francisco, Los Angeles Festival director Peter Sellars attacked *Africa Oyé* as "vilely produced. Eight major groups of artists were slung together in a kind of smorgasbord treatment," he said. "Just imagine us sending to Africa a show saying, 'Hello, this is Western Culture.' And we would send five minutes of *La Bohème*, and a fifteen-minute excerpt of *Swan Lake* . . . and that's the 'American Show,' and we'll take that around Africa. I mean, the idea is so demeaning: 'Now let's look at Africa through a series of fifteen-minute excerpts of major artists.'"

Interviewed by this writer, *Africa Oyé* producer and codirector Mel Howard replied to Sellars' charges by saying, "We did not excerpt anything. Every piece in the show is complete. There were time constraints but we were very careful and asked the artists for whole pieces that did not deform a larger or longer work." On the "smorgasbord" issue, he said, "Despite using diverse elements, my goal was to make a piece of theater that felt seamless. It took us two years to find groups that would create the proper chemistry for the evening."

Why not longer performances by fewer groups? "I don't think an audience that will be coming to see this show in huge theaters would want to sit through forty-five minutes of most of the groups," he answered. "When we can't understand what they're singing, it could seem repetitive if it went on too long." Again, it depends on whom you ask.

Obviously, producing any dance tour is a high-risk proposition in the recessionary 1990s, but countless unexplored formats exist between the extremes of the two-hour tourist hodgepodge and the all-night, torchlight-and-moths festival for purists. The most modest could easily be adopted for the very next tour to hit these shores. What would happen, for instance, if the Oyé Africans or Namgyal Tibetans or Folklórico Chileans dropped the variety-show approach after intermission and devoted Act 2 to a single piece performed in something like documentary real-time? Would American audiences run shrieking into the night? Of course not. The generation that cut its teeth on postmodernism could just be the best prepared in our history to meet the structures and time schemes of the most daunting world dance idioms, without compromise. Or, at least, with *less* compromise.

The potpourri, at best, represents an introductory paradigm, and after so many introductions, it's high time for attempts at genuine acquaintance. But how? Even the most familiar touring companies (Ballet Folklórico de México, Bayanihan, Moiseyev) offer only a changing array of highlights from season to season. Moreover, Sellars' own 1990 Los Angeles Festival resorted to plenty of smorgasbord programming, with three Native American groups sharing one evening and three Oceanic groups another at a UCLA venue, and with the Classical Dance Company of Cambodia presenting sampler repertory at the Los Angeles Arboretum.

In each case, Sellars utilized familiar Euro-American modes of dance presentation quite at odds with the way native

Les Ballets Africains from The Republic of Guinea, photo © Jack Vartoogian

audiences might encounter these dances in ideal situations at their points of origin. The UCLA programs resembled "mixed bills" of modern dance or ballet, while the Cambodians appeared in something like a divertissement—*Ramayana Variations*, perhaps. Moreover, the assumptions about the American audience remained exactly the same as Mel Howard's, Geiogamah's, or those of distinguished Javanese classical choreographer R. Rio Sasminta Mardawa.

"The Western attention span is two hours," Mardawa declared to visiting journalists in Yogyakarta in the summer of 1990, speaking with the unshakable surety of a prophet citing the *Koran* or *Bhagavad Gita*. His task at that moment: preparing the Court Art of Java repertory for American consumption on a Festival of Indonesia tour. No wonder the company's *Wayang Wong Mahabharata* proved heavily abridged here, more linear and plot-bound than audiences find it back home and, as such, more American. Peter Brook can bring a nine-hour *Mahabharata* to the United States, but Mardawa and his counterparts have come to feel they must play by a different set of rules.

At least Los Angeles Festival audiences saw the *Wayang Wong* at close range on the Arboretum's outdoor platform stage. With bleacher seating for 869 flanking the sides of the playing area, this space scarcely resembled the elegant dance pavilions in the sultan's *kraton* (palace), but it proved infinitely preferable to the large proscenium theaters that the company encountered later on the tour.

Los Angeles arts writer, novelist, and performer Douglas Sadownick saw the complete Court Art of Java repertory at the Arboretum and then caught a performance at the 2,100-seat Brooklyn Academy of Music some ten days later. "It was a totally different experience," he said. "There was a real distance between performers and audience—as if you were looking at postcards. It was dead on that [BAM] stage. Everyone around me was sleeping and if I had seen it there for the first time, I wouldn't have found it interesting at all." David Gere (former dance critic of *The Oakland Tribune*) and Rhoda Grauer (creator of the PBS series *Dancing*) have reported similar responses to the Javanese changes of venue.

Consider that dance spaces are as culturally determined as dance itself, and the proscenium theater exists primarily to serve pictorial illusion and crowd control. Idioms with other priorities can be at a loss there, but seeking alternative contexts not only runs afoul of the practicalities of theatrical real estate but also of several kinds of elitism. Audience responses to a panel at the 1990 San Francisco Ethnic Dance Festival and discussions with some of Sellars' Los Angeles Festival advisers confirmed that many world dance artists want opera-house bookings due to the status involved. Dancing under the velvet drapes and chandeliers of a U.S. culture mall represents a genuine political victory: the takeover of a Euro-American symbol of high art by traditions struggling to be respected. What earth-stage or plaza, however inviting, can deliver as much—especially when our cultural power brokers validate that line of thinking?

"Folk art has always needed the mediation of the theatre," wrote Arlene Croce in the July 23, 1990, issue of *The New Yorker.* "Without the theatre, dance isn't a medium, it's the preserve of anthropologists, not of artists."

Significantly, Croce never addresses the question of which theater, whose theater. The dance pavilions at the *kraton* in Yogyakarta are definitely theaters, but if the dances that belong to them can't survive the mediation of the Brooklyn Academy of Music, why not house them more appropriately? No, you don't have to create an architectural replica of any palace or temple, merely conditions that provide maximum access to the dance experience on its own terms. It can be as simple as publishing translations of song-texts in the program booklet or as complex as prompting Croce and kindred spirits to expand their definitions of "the theater," dance as "a medium," and which dancers can be considered "artists."

Would Croce accept the cafés and caves where flamenco evolved as theaters—or does this idiom need the mediation of a proscenium house where, most of the time, the guitar-and-vocal complement is amplified and the heelwork is not? Without denying flamenco (or any dance idiom) the right to grow beyond its original environment, can't we acknowledge that the satisfactions it offers drastically shift once the primacy of heelwork erodes and music becomes dominant?

Obviously, flamenco belongs to European culture, but the problems of inappropriate performance contexts don't vanish as we embrace homegrown repertory. Indeed, one can argue that they color our reactions to everything from the Romantic ballets of August Bournonville to the early dance dramas of both Antony Tudor and Martha Graham. Moreover, our experimental choreographers continually challenge entrenched Euro-American norms of theatrical scale, duration, audience proximity, and performance structure—exactly the norms that so often corrupt world dance on Western stages.

A young dance student once approached the Los Angeles Times about writing freelance reviews. He could see bodies brilliantly—their weaknesses, their capacities—but he saw choreography only through the prism of ballet. For him, world dance was preballet or wanna-be ballet and modern dance antiballet or wanna-be ballet. He simply couldn't perceive the parity of other traditions, including alternate visions of classicism, and much of the world dance we might show him in a typical season would only empower his condescension. It is like looking at postcards, or Tudor's Dark Elegies at the Met. It is often balleticized to an alarming extent—not merely the Eastern European ensembles but some in Asia and Latin America as well.

On tour in 1990, for example, Ballet Folklórico Nacional de Chile opened its suite from Easter Island with a display of the kind of nude-look leotards and weightless, linear jumps (with pointed toes, of course) you'd expect to find in a provincial production of an exotic opera such as *Aïda* or *Lakmé*. In all its fundamental assumptions, this scandalous ethnographic charade was about American entertainment, not some Polynesian "other": a reflection of the celluloid fantasies some of us picked up in movie houses about brown-skinned primitives going into their dance.

Clearly, mere accommodation isn't accommodating enough these days. The politics of multiculturalism may extort extravagant hymns to diversity from everyone, but more and more that perceptual filter between us and the traditional cultures we think we're seeing on our stages looks suspiciously like a mirror.

From: LOOKING OUT:
Perspectives on
Dance & Criticism
in a Multicult. Wld.

Ed: David Gere

Prentice Hall 1995

Nicole Plett
Vicky Holt Takamine
Sardono W. Kusumo
R.M. Soedarsono
Peter Nabokov
Julia Pardoe
Kapila Vatsyayan

NICOLE PLETT: When a dance critic sets out to attend a performance—usually under cover of darkness—the destination is bound to influence both preparation and expectations. We know our theaters as places of heightened awareness, each with its own shape, scale, and feel. Will the dance unfold in the neoclassical splendor of the Brooklyn Academy? At the elegant Mark Taper Forum? Or in the casual intimacy of a dancer's downtown loft? These are things dance critics think about when they set out to give a dance work their fullest attention.

But there is another kind of performing space which is also a place of heightened awareness: this is the sacred space of ritual dance. Perhaps today's critics can take comfort in the knowledge that all dance was originally sacred. Indeed, throughout the world people have danced, and continue to dance, with a sacred purpose. Dances have long been performed to acquire food, to honor the dead, or to assure good order in the cosmos. Such performances can be occasions of solemnity, of celebration, and of community bonding.

◀ *Auntie Edith Kanaka'ole chanting in the koa forest, Kipuka Puaula, Volcano, Hawai'i, 1977, photo © Franco Salmoiraghi*

Traditional dances are intimately connected to the places, people, and landscapes that nurture them. Where dance is integral to a culture and its liturgy, performances often take place in sacred spaces. These are spaces that have been, or will be, visited by deities; they mark the birth sites of holy figures, prophets, or visionaries, and are related to important events in their mortal lives. They are sanctified by generations of use and by community belief. Such "home spaces" have unique qualities; they may be distinguished not only by natural beauty, but also by their spirit—which philosopher Gaston Bachelard would call "the poetics of space."

There is no single definition of sacred space; its shapes and forms are myriad. Sacred space may be an outdoor temple nestled high above the Pacific surf in Hawai'i or a temporary, symbolic enclosure erected in an Indian village. Sacred space may be embodied within the performer, as in Javanese *Bedhaya*, or it may take the form of a dance plaza or "arbor," one element of the American Pueblo Indians' sacred universe.

I have been asked why dance writers should care about sacred spaces. Here are a few possibilities. The most obvious is to be able to understand and to observe the behavior that is customary and "natural" there. More significantly, an appreciation of sacred geography and architecture opens our experience to space as an active player in performance. It can also lead us to think about how dance can act as a conduit between spatial and conceptual realms.

In one of Peter Nabokov's essays he describes a conversation between an Ojibwa tribesman and an anthropologist who has posed the question, "Are all rocks alive?"

"No," replied the Ojibwa, but, writes Nabokov, all could be. More importantly, rocks, trees, mountains, and caves that became "alive" also attained the status of "person"—and, thus, responsible interaction with such "persons" was a mark of good citizenship in Ojibwa cultural relations.

Similarly, we might ask ourselves, Are our stages "alive"? Are the lofts and amphitheaters and halls where we often see dance "alive"? What part does space play in the culture of which we—as dance writers, choreographers, performers—are citizens?

Considering the question of space inevitably involves us in the process through which ritual dances are transported from their home environments—from their "sacred geography"—to the performance venues in which American audiences most frequently encounter them. The implications of such acts of transplantation are immense.

These are the kinds of issues that scholars and practitioners of what we call "traditional" dance forms are well suited to contemplate. What, then, is the space where such dance occurs, and how is sacred space properly recognized, honored, and described?

HAWAI'I, POLYNESIA

VICKY HOLT TAKAMINE: Ka-ulu-Pā'oa *heiau*, a temple on the island of Kaua'i, was built by high chief Lohi'au and dedicated to Laka, goddess of the hula. This particular temple went into decline about 1819, at a time when many *heiau* were being destroyed by Christianized Hawaiians. Even so, the *kumu hula* (master teachers) of the island continue to visit it. The temple consists of several levels. The upper level was the site of a *hālau* hula school, a thatched structure where dancers were trained. One level below this *hālau* structure was the open performance space.

Inside the *hālau* was an altar that held a piece of lama wood, draped with yellow *kapa*, or bark cloth. Dancers were sent into the forest, the domain of the goddess Laka, to gather greenery—ferns and flowers—to adorn the altar, chanting as they decorated it. The most basic *hālau* ceremony involves dressing the dancer in a skirt of yellow *kapa* (similar to that draped on the altar), wristlets, anklets, and *lei* for the neck and for the

Ka-ulu-Pā'oa heiau, Kaua'i, photo © Franco Salmoiraghi

head. For each item, the dancer performs a chant invoking the presence of the gods in the altar as well as in the body. Only after this ceremony is the dancer allowed to proceed to the performance space.

Ka-ulu-Pā'oa *heiau* is being restored, a difficult process since so much of Hawaiian culture has been lost. In the oral tradition, our history and our culture were transmitted from generation to generation through legends, in the form of chants. But when the Christian missionaries arrived in the early 1800s, confronting Hawaiians with both a new religion and a new social structure, many traditional ways were deemed "pagan." As a result, much of our culture and history vanished.

Like many of our temples, Ka-ulu-Pā'oa *heiau* is situated on a high bluff that overlooks the ocean, surrounded by the sounds of wind and ocean surf. Because Hawaiians are worshippers of nature, these sounds are extremely important; they encourage the dancer to be attuned to everything around her. Since all the resources are here—the mountains, the greenery, and the sounds and forces of nature—it is an ideal place for training.

Leona Kahawaiola'a at Ka'ana, Moloka'i, photo by Philip Spalding III

Equally ideal is a spot called Ka'ana, a holy place on the island of Moloka'i on top of Maunaloa mountain. From there you can see the ocean and the island of Lāna'i in the distance. According to Moloka'i tradition, Ka'ana was the birthplace of the goddess Laka. Born mortal, she was a master dancer and teacher of the renowned hula school on this site. According to tradition, she was deified after her death.

A grove of *lehua*—a type of tree associated with the goddess Pele—used to grow here. But goats and cattle introduced from America destroyed the trees, leaving Ka'ana a barren hillside. Nonetheless, it remains a Moloka'i tradition to honor the goddess Laka in this place.

By contrast, a third site for sacred dance is a dance platform constructed at Moanalua Gardens on the island of O'ahu named Kama'ipu'upa'a for the close companion of Prince Lot, Kamehameha V. It is a grassy raised platform in a grove of trees built for the Prince Lot Hula Festival in about 1980. Incredibly, it is bounded on one side by a freeway and a shopping center, with a subdivision behind it. However, when

Pua Ali'i 'Ilima hālau performing at Kama'ipu'upa'a, Moanalua Gardens, O'ahu,
photo by Joe Bear Carini

you watch hula here, you are transported into another era, hardly aware of the urban setting.

Although physical sacred spaces are essential to our tradition, there is another kind of sacred space that is just as important. Through the dressing ceremony I described earlier, each dancer becomes her own altar, which means that she takes her sacred space with her wherever she performs.

When I graduated as *kumu hula*, for example, the ceremony was held on a hillside at Pūpūkea, O'ahu. It was not a sacred area, so we had to prepare the space, as well as ourselves. We chanted throughout the night with our teacher. Then there was a *pī kai*, the ceremony for purification. In the *'ailolo* ceremony, a black pig was cooked in an underground oven and all of its parts were eaten. Symbolically, the brains were consumed for knowledge, the ears for hearing, the eyes for sight, the feet for nimbleness of hands and feet, and the tail and the snout for humbleness of self. After the meal, we dressed for our performance in a private ceremony. Only then were we allowed to go out and share the dances and chants we had learned as part of our training.

In making *Kumu Hula: Keepers of a Culture*, a documentary that I coproduced with Robert Mugge, we chose 'Ulupalakua on the island of Maui as one of our "locations." It is not a sacred place, but the dancers, the chanter, and the teacher made it so. After the dancers were dressed, the *kumu hula* gathered all of us together and asked us to pray. Although we may now pray to a different God than our ancestors did, we are still requesting the same things—strength of voice and nimbleness of hands and feet—and giving thanks for blessings received. On this occasion, we gave thanks for the history and the culture that had been passed on to us, for the belief in our ancestors, and for their legacy to us. Everyone took part: the dancers, their parents, the *kumu*, even the film crew. Then they performed the sacred dance 'Au'a Ia, which means "hold fast":

> Hold fast, oh child, to your heritage
> To your heritage child, hold on
> Oh child of the turning tides, child of the
>   changing times
> Observe the passing of things that will
>   be no more

JAVA, INDONESIA

SARDONO W. KUSUMO: During the 1990 Festival of Indonesia, many Americans became familiar with the *Bedhaya Arjuna Wiwaha*, a seventeeth-century dance from the court of Yogyakarta, which is one of two main centers of Javanese culture. Although a spiritual atmosphere is evident in the performance, this *Bedhaya* is not considered the most sacred of such forms. In Yogyakarta, the most sacred *Bedhaya* is no longer known and cannot be traced. In Surakarta, however, the second cultural center, the ritual *Bedhaya Ketawang* is still performed for a limited audience on the anniversary of the coronation of the *Sunan* (king) of Surakarta.

About two hours in duration, this sacred *Bedhaya Ketawang* is different from the *Bedhaya Arjuna Wiwaha*. Its impulses are more poetic and meditative, its music, costumes, and lighting are simpler, its movements more flowing. During *Bedhaya Ketawang*, it is believed that, in addition to the nine dancers, a tenth dancer may materialize. She is the Goddess of the South Sea. Today, the performance retinue may include relatives of the *Sunan* as well as students of the dance academies. But in former times, it was taboo for a daughter of the king to be present with the Goddess of the South Sea. Such things are changing.

Rehearsal times for the *Bedhaya* are ritualized. The days for practice are prescribed according to the convergence of the lunar calendar of seven weekdays and an older indigenous calendar of five weekdays. Thus every thirty-fifth day is

Wayang Wong at the Yogyakarta palace, photo © Linda Vartoogian

auspicious. Although the *pendhapa*, or pavilion, is the usual site, *Bedhaya* can be performed in other spaces and still be sacred, so long as it is still related to the court ritual.

Java does not seem to have specific sacred places per se, probably because of the admixture of Hinduism, Buddhism, and Islam in our tradition. Bali, in contrast, has sacred temples which are sites for dance in each community and often within a residential compound. In Java there are no sacred places designated especially for dance, but each house has an anterooom that functions as quasi-sacred space. It is my opinion that Javanese dance makes *all* things sacred.

R.M. SOEDARSONO: Until the eve of World War I, Javanese court dance remained a ritual court activity, and nobody outside the palace could learn it. In 1918, two revolutionary princes—Prince Tedjakusuma and Prince Surjodiningrat—brought Javanese dance outside the palace for the first time, allowing anybody to be instructed in the techniques. Why? Because they believed that from learning Javanese dance we could also learn Javanese etiquette, ethics, morals, and the stories of our legendary ancestors. In this way, Javanese dance became a part of Javanese education for children, especially among the aristocrats. I learned Javanese dance not from the dance academies but as part of my regular education. It was believed that every child who thought of him- or herself as Javanese should know how to dance these dances.

In most Javanese court dance-rituals, the ritual is connected with ancestor worship or with the special link between the king and the spiritual queen of the South Sea. In our mythology, when the first king of Java was crowned, the Goddess of the South Sea promised to help him whenever he needed. But, in return, the king was required to agree to marry her in a kind of spiritual marriage. This ritual is reenacted by each new king, which is why the *Bedhaya* is always performed after a coronation. Each new king also creates another *Bedhaya*, however, which is less sacred but still ritualistic and can be performed for the celebration of the birthday of the sultan, for the wedding ceremonies of the sons and daughters of the sultan, and for dance-dramas in which the legends of our ancestors are enacted. That is why everybody is allowed to see these performances—because the people of Java and Jakarta are not just the audience but also the congregation. Watching the performance is not just education; the people expect to receive a spiritual blessing from the performance. Even when it is so crowded that everybody in the audience is not able to see the performance, everyone is satisfied just to be there and to belong to the congregation.

HOPI, NATIVE AMERICA

PETER NABOKOV: As religious and social havens of Pueblo Indians everywhere, kivas are the oldest type of religious buildings in continuous use in the Western Hemisphere. Their location—often sunk halfway into the earth like their pit house prototype—intentionally suggested a link between this world and the ancestral underworld with its manifold benevolent powers. In many kivas the old *sipapu* shrine was maintained; among the Hopi it was covered by a cottonwood board that dancers could stomp upon to send messages to the spirits below.

Kivas have many forms and functions. What is known about them is mostly conjectural, however, due to the cloak of secrecy around Pueblo religious beliefs and practices. Hopi kivas are generally about twenty-five feet long, fifteen feet wide, and ten feet high, with a third of the floor space raised half a foot or more so that an audience can watch performances from

A version of this text first appeared in Peter Nabokov and Robert Easton, *Native American Architecture* (New York: Oxford University Press, 1989). Reprinted by permission of the author.

behind the leaning entry ladder. Wood stoves near the ladder warm the rooms, and nearby is the covered *sipapu* hole. In most Hopi communities, each of the village clans and religious societies has its own kiva. Wherever possible they are oriented north-south, although some mesa-top sites are too narrow.

At Acoma Pueblo, west of present-day Albuquerque, New Mexico, an origin myth tells of the First Kiva. A culture hero declares, "We have no sacred place. ... This is the way I emerged, so I guess we will make a house in the ground ... this will be a sacred place for the kachina when they come." The first Acomans learned how to design this circular kiva so that it resembled their emergence place, but it also symbolized the entire world. Its four beams were drawn from the first four trees to stand on Earth, and its roof stood for the Milky Way. The walls were "the sky," and four hollows in the walls stood for the "doors" of Acoma's four sacred mountains. Encircling the chamber was a bench, or *banco*, which stood for the fog where the rain-giving kachina spirits dwelled. When descending the tilting ladder, which represented a rainbow, one faced the rungs, because to look down shortened life.

Nearly all of these sacred structures are off-limits to nonresidents, and many a tourist has been sternly reproached, even by young children, for failing to observe the prohibition against taking photographs or trespassing. They remain the most potent architectural reminder of the abiding gulf between Pueblo and Anglo-American worldviews.

In mid-February 1990, I had a rare opportunity to watch the Hopi kivas serve their ancient function as theaters for sacred performance. The sole occasion when outsiders can enter these charged chambers occurs during the Bean Dance, a segment of the great *Powamuy* festival, which takes place in midwinter. The public events of the Bean Dance include a parade by more than a hundred kachinas through the Pueblo streets and alleys, with kachina dancing and intricately staged puppet ceremonies in the kivas throughout the night. It is only on the last night of the sixteen-day festival, we were told, that nonresidents are permitted to witness the kiva rituals.

When we ascended First Mesa in late afternoon, we learned that each of its nine kivas was responsible for producing one "act," which circulated from kiva to kiva. If we found a good berth in one kiva, we could enjoy all nine of the mesa's performances. At first we tried to get a good seat in a Walpi kiva, but its townsfolk were anxious that their own women and children might not have enough standing room in their exceedingly small kivas, so we huddled in the sleet and rain around a Sichomovi ladder well, which looked down as if into a well-lit cave. On the roof beams we noticed fresh hand smears

indicating the last plasterers' prayers for rain.

In six of the acts, teams of kachina dancers wearing identical animal masks filled the stage floor, singing and shuffling in time to shaking rattles. Between their performances, three classic puppet acts were presented. During intermissions, the Coleman lanterns were turned low and hooded, and we were brusquely whisked away from the kiva hatchways by masked Wuyataywas, or Angry Guard Kachinas. Under cover of darkness the staging for the next act was dropped into the kiva and made ready. At a signal, illumination flooded the interior once more, accompanied by renewed singing, drumming, and whirling colors. Each puppet show, which dramatized folkloristic figures and stories primarily meant to entertain and teach the women and children, opened against a screen vividly painted

Butterfly Dance, San Ildefonso Pueblo, c. 1935, photo by T. Harmon Parkhurst,
courtesy Museum of New Mexico, negative number 3629

with cloud, lightning, and rain symbols, and bordered by young fir trees which had recently been harvested from a sacred grove.

In the third of these performances was a piece of puppetry which, we were told, had not been enacted on First Mesa for decades. It depicted the Sa'lakwmanawyat, or Corn Grinding Maidens—two figures beloved to the Hopi. When the kiva lights flared on, the little girls seemed merely painted on a screen which stretched from wall to wall of the kiva, flanked by fir trees. Then their little arms stuck out from the backdrop and began swaying in rhythm to music by means of strings pulled by their invisible puppeteers.

Suddenly the masked chorus of kachina dancers on either side thronged toward the girls, momentarily blocking them from our view. When they drew back the girls seemed alive, their tablita headdresses tipping forward as they knelt over miniature stone *metates* and began to grind corn.

White-daubed, clownlike kachinas, who gleefully clapped their hands and adoringly attended to the little girls, squatted on the kiva floor and took pinches of their newly ground cornmeal to sprinkle on the heads of recently initiated youngsters in the front row of the audience. Then the kiva was sunk in darkness. When the lights reappeared, only the clowns lay curled on the dirt floor, apparently heartbroken at the loss of the dolls. Comforted by the children, they hobbled up the kiva ladder. Without fanfare, the show abruptly ended there, and the lanterns were doused for the last time.

Our final glance was into a murky interior, where kiva members with headbands and flashlights were shooing visitors and breaking down the set. Steam from departing bodies lingered over the ladder well. Then a kiva official ordered us out of the way as he tugged the wood-and-tarpaper hatchcover and sealed the kiva.

ISTANBUL, TURKEY

JULIA PARDOE: I paid two visits to the convent of Turning, or as they are commonly called in Europe, Dancing Dervishes, which is situated opposite the Petit Champs Des Morts, descending towards Galata. The court of the Tekie is entered by a handsomely ornamented gate and having passed it, you have the cemetery of the brethren on your left hand, and the gable of the main building on your right. As you arrive in front of the convent, the court widens, and in the midst stands a magnificent tree of great antiquity, carefully railed in; while you have on one side the elegant mausoleum in which repose the superiors of the order; and on the other the fountain of white marble, roofed in like an oratory, and enclosed on all its six sides from the weather, where the Dervishes perform their ablutions ere they enter the chapel. The mausoleum is of the octagon form, the floor being raised two steps in the centre, leaving a space all around, just sufficiently wide for one person to pass along. The sarcophagi are covered with plain clay-coloured cloth, and at the head of each tomb is placed the genlaf, or Dervishes hat, encircled by a clear muslim handkerchief embroidered with tinted silks and gold thread. . . . Huge wax candles in plain clay-coloured candlesticks are scattered among the tombs.

The chapel is an octagon building of moderate size, neatly painted in fresco. The centre of the floor is railed off, and the enclosure is sacred to the brotherhood; while the outer circle, covered with Indian matting, is appropriated to visitors. A deep gallery runs round six sides of the building, and beneath it, on your left hand as you enter, you remark the lattices through which the Turkish women witness the service. A narrow mat surrounds the circle within the railing and upon this the brethren kneel during the prayers; while the centre of the floor is so

Excerpted from *The City of the Sultan*, 2 vols. (London: Henry Colburn, 1837).

highly polished by the perpetual friction that it resembles a mirror and the boards are united by nails with heads as large as a shilling to prevent accidents to the feet of the Dervishes during their evolutions. A bar of iron descends octagonally from the centre of the domed roof, to which transverse bars are attached, bearing a large number of glass lamps of different colours and sizes; and against many of the pillars, of which I counted four and twenty, supporting the dome, are hung frames, within which are inscribed passages from the Prophets.

Above the seat of the superior, the name of the founder of the Tekie is written in gold on a black ground in immense characters. This seat consists of a small carpet, above which is spread a crimson rug, and on this the worthy principal was squatted when we entered, in an ample cloak of Spanish brown, with large hanging sleeves, and his genlaf, or high hat of gray felt, encircled with a green shawl. I pitied him that his back was turned towards the glorious Bosphorus, that was distinctly seen through the four large windows at the extremity of the chapel, flashing in the light, with the slender minarets and lordly mosques of Stamboul gleaming out in the distance.

Dervishes, Istanbul, Turkey, photo courtesy "Baraka"

One by one the Dervishes entered the chapel, bowing profoundly at the little gate of the enclosure, took their places on the mat and bending down, reverently kissed the ground; and then, folding their arms meekly on their breasts, remained buried in prayer, with their eyes closed and their bodies swaying slowly to and fro. They were all enveloped in wide cloaks of dark coloured cloth with pendant sleeves; and wore their genlafs, which they retained during the whole of the service.

There was a deep stillness, broken only by the breath of prayer or the melancholy wailing of the muffled instruments, which seemed to send forth their voice of sadness from behind a cloud in subdued sorrowing, like the melodious plaint of angels over fallen mortality—the concentrated and pious self-forgetfulness of the community, who never once cast their eyes over the crowds that thronged their chapel. . . .

Immediately after passing with a solemn reverence, twice performed, the place of the High Priest, who remained standing, the Dervishes spread their arms and commenced their revolving motion; the palm of the right hand being held upwards, and that of the left downwards. Their under dresses consisted of a jacket and petticoat of dark coloured cloth, that descended to their feet; the higher order of brethren being clad in green, and the others in brown, or a sort of yellowish gray; about their waists they wore girdles, edged with red, to which the right side of the jacket was closely fastened, while the left hung loose; their petticoats were of immense width and laid in large plaits, beneath the girdle, and, as the wearers swung around, formed a bell-like appearance; these latter garments are worn only during the ceremony, and are exchanged in summer for white ones of lighter material.

The number of those who were "on duty," was nine; seven of them being men and the remaining two, mere boys, the youngest certainly not more than ten years old. . . . So true and unerring were their motions that, although the space which they occupied was somewhat circumscribed, they never once gained upon each other and for five minutes they continued twirling round and round, as though impelled by machinery, their pale passionless countenances perfectly immobile, their heads slightly declined towards the right shoulder, and their inflated garments creating a cold, sharp air in the chapel from the rapidity of their action. At the termination of that period, the name of the Prophet occurred in the chant, which had been unintermitted in the gallery; and, as they simultaneously paused, and, folding their hands upon their breasts, bent down in reverence at the sound, their ample garments wound about them at the sudden check. An interval of prayer followed; and the same ceremony performed three times.

MANIPUR, INDIA

KAPILA VATSYAYAN: All ancient civilizations and many contemporary societies have organized space, established a physical center, made enclosures, and then invested those enclosures with magic and cosmic significance. I consider the proscenium stage, or any performing area, for that matter, to be sacred for a certain time and duration. Therefore, it is part of my training not to bring shoes and dirt onto the stage. The stage is both a sacred and a most demanding mistress. I think any dancer knows this.

In all cases, the inner space is that of the heart. The outer space is that of material, physical space. These are in communion through consciousness. This urge for communion manifests itself in more permanent structures—temples, amphitheaters, cathedrals, pyramids, ziggurats, caves, and stupas. These habitations and monuments are an expression of consecrated space and thus are meant to lead man to that experience of wholeness and totality which he sometimes loses. Within these structures, he creates strategies by which reintegration can be affirmed. This experience consists of an inner silent contemplation, during which all energies are concentrated within, differentiations are lost, and individuals merge. For a specific time and duration he calls this physical space or his physical surroundings "sacred."

Monuments—"dead matter," so to speak—become enlivened when they are given breath and life. In some instances enlivening comes through the consecration of an image; in others, in a great temple gathering.

Whether in architecture or in dance, the identification of the "center" is primary and essential. That center is the navel of the body; it is the womb-house around which all sacredness is recreated. An enclosure can be created physically or conceptually; an area does not need bricks to demarcate it. It can be celestial space, the space where the process of transformation begins—for he who performs and for he who witnesses. An instance of this transformation is found at Manipur, in the hills of northeastern India.

In Manipur, dance is central. It is not performance; it is part of the passage of life. It is connected with the seasons; it is connected with myths and legends. I want to describe one among hundreds of such events, namely the Sankirtana.

First, a center is established. A *mandap*, or enclosure, is made as the participants watch. A bamboo stalk or a tree trunk can become a sacred tree; the moment of its placement establishes the center. This "pillar" then symbolizes the axis mundi. It is the wish tree, the relationship of earth to heaven. It is also the body of man from foot to head, connecting earth to heaven.

Around the pillar is the enclosure, within which the cardinal points or directions are established. Then the performance begins, led by a person we may call the "director"; he is the empowered individual. Near the middle pillar at the western side, facing east, sits the conch blower. The conch shell provides

The ritual Sankirtana, Manipur, India,
photo courtesy Kapila Vatsyayan

the primeval sound, the *adhinada*—the first manifestation of form.

A little farther away from the performing area at the north-west corner is an enclosure for the officiating priest. He signifies the chief of the devotees. Metaphorically, this expresses the relationship of Krishna to his devotees—Krishna as the Principle of the One and the devotees as the Principle of the Many. Women sit at the north and western side of the performing area, while men occupy the south and the eastern side. Thus the choreography is very set in terms of space.

After the ceremony begins, no performer or audience member can leave that enclosure. The officiating priest consecrates the tree, which becomes the deity. Clothes are offered, both to the pillar and to the performers on behalf of all those who take part. The observance is divided into five sequentially arranged sections and lasts from five to seven hours. Normally there are sixteen male dancers divided into two groups. The leader of the first group sings the first line; a respondent leads the second group. One group moves clockwise, the other counter-clockwise.

The two drummers are most important. There is a text, but it is the drumming and the change of the raga that comprise the invocation. For that time and duration, all the performers are transformed into the Female Principle; the pillar is the Male Principle. After a crescendo of drumming, the flowering and renewal of life on earth are re-established and the universe is presented again—the universe of plants and animals and birds; of men and women; and of all living matter. The event involves total participation, with complete dedication and merging of individual entities into a collective totality, a dialogue of the center and the periphery.

Space is consecrated; so is time. A light is lit. The "director" of the performance gives the sign and, once the offerings are distributed, the site returns to mundane space.

Allegra Fuller Snyder

That the Hollywood worldview has played a fundamental role in shaping twentieth-century thought, both in the United States and around the world, is not a new insight. Gilbert Seldes first proposed the idea in his *The 7 Lively Arts*, written in 1924, and Gore Vidal's 1992 *Screening History* also focuses on Hollywood's power.[1] When, however, we begin specifically to question how Hollywood has affected our attitudes toward and our understanding of dance—particularly world dance—then we *are* addressing something new.

Even for those of us who had long believed in the importance of this topic, the body of material necessary to undertake a thorough study had not been easily available, despite the existence of such major film archives as those at UCLA, the Academy of Motion Picture Arts and Sciences, and the Museum of Modern Art. Only recently—since most major films have found their way onto video (some of them illegally) and have been made available for personal use—could we bring the realm of Hollywood films into our own studies. In nearly every major modern city, there is now a place like North Hollywood's "Eddie Brandt's Saturday Matinee," which professes to have virtually every Hollywood film available on video. Thanks to such resources, Hollywood materials can

The author wishes to thank Howie Davidson and Becky Stone for their tireless and invaluable assistance.

1.   Seldes (New York: Harper & Bros., 1924); Vidal (Cambridge, Mass.: Harvard University Press, 1992).

◄   *Betty Grable in "Song of the Islands,"* 1942, © *Twentieth Century Fox Film Corp.*

now become a more central part of our concerns. Video anthropology is now a process in which any dance researcher can engage.

Admittedly, I began with strong notions about what the Hollywood material would reveal. I had thought I would uncover clear Hollywood biases, misconceptions, and prejudices in dealing with all non-American-based dance forms and cultural expressions. I soon realized, however, that I was at least as biased as I thought Hollywood had been. In any ethnographic investigation, the material tells its own story and reveals its own meanings. What I discovered were attitudes with much softer edges than I had expected. Some films were simply naïve. Others were apprehensive, fearful, or indulged in overly romanticized approaches to dealing with the Other. In many instances I found that a specific geographical area elicited a generic response to that area and that the generic response to Asia was different from the generic response to the Pacific Island areas, which was different still from the response to South America. These generalized attitudes seemed to characterize an overarching approach taken by filmmakers to particular bodies of material, even though within each "generic" approach lay a range of subtle and not-so-subtle variations.

My background in dance ethnology proved helpful in identifying and defining the contextual and choreographic biases present in Hollywood interpretations of world dance, but this did not lead me to conclude that Hollywood was presenting a stereotypical point of view. Rather, Hollywood seemed to have genuinely struggled with this issue—sometimes picturing the Other in a negative light, sometimes making the Other suit its expectations or needs. In either case, the spectrum of approaches was broad. The central problem seemed to be a lack of critical knowledge, evaluation, and understanding of the material from the point of view of the members of the culture being represented. But even in that regard, some interesting changes may be taking place.

For this project, two assistants (Howie Davidson and Becky Stone) and I spent some four months reviewing Hollywood film resources, which turned out to be barely enough time to get started. That time constraint alone makes the results of our work tentative and in no way either inclusive or conclusive. Each week we gathered for some four to six hours, "fast-forwarding" through feature films. Fast-forwarding is an interesting tool that alters perception and is a research technique that I strongly recommend to others engaged in video or film analysis. Moving quickly through the images, one gains a strong sense of larger visual patterns. These are, of course, divorced from the soundtrack and therefore stand out more clearly on their own. Through this method the significance of an image is quickly captured.

As we began to view the more than eighty films included in our research—and to create our reservoir of resources—ideas and patterns gradually emerged. In order to create realistic parameters for our task, we limited our selections to the "Pan-Pacific" area—by which we meant, by current definition, all cultures surrounding the Pacific Ocean (Asia, South America, and the western coast of North America, including indigenous Native American groups in that area). At the same time, we recognized the importance of taking at least a brief look at the famous "Tarzan" films to uncover generalized approaches to "the primitive"—generic patterns that Hollywood might resort to regardless of locale.

Indeed, there is a rich amount of material on the "exotic" Pacific area as seen through Hollywood eyes, some of which epitomizes the cultural confusions inherent in Hollywood's most bizarre images of world dance. Eleanor Powell's "tap hula" in *Honolulu* (1939) is a prime example. But Hollywood sometimes hired accomplished, culturally sensitive choreographers to present pan–Pacific dances, too, notably Lester Horton (e.g., *Rhythm of the Islands*, 1943) and Katherine Dunham (e.g., *Pardon My Sarong*, 1942). What had these choreographers done with their material?

The role of the choreographer is, in fact, central to an exploration of Hollywood's approaches to world dance. Many traditional dance forms are not "choreographed" but emerge and are reformulated as a part of the cultural process. When this process is altered and put into the hands of a choreographer, a whole new set of considerations presents itself. If the choreographer can wear two hats, that of ethnographer as well as dancemaker, the sensitivity to the material and to its reformulation will have much more integrity than if it is simply treated as a creative challenge or commercial commodity. When the choreographer ultimately has very little say in the matter, however, as is true in the majority of Hollywood films, the research shows that the integrity of the process is particularly at risk. Had Horton and Dunham, for example, felt the pressure of Hollywood in making their cultural as well as aesthetic choices?

Evoking the Primitive

Historically, Hollywood's most fundamentally negative approach to world dance has been reserved for indigenous peoples, a group that seems to exist for filmmakers in a generic, non-culture-specific category coded simply as "primitive." *Tarzan and the Leopard Woman* (1946), with choreography by Lester Horton, is a quintessential example of this basic Hollywood misrepresentation. The dance sequences are stereotypically identified by their "primitive" qualities, such as hunched-over bodies and heavy, pounding feet. Almost by definition, in other words, "primitive" people are those who practice "primitive" dancing. Such stereotypic movements are particularly instrumental in *Tarzan*, where the act of dancing translates into a vague sense that the "natives" are restless. An overtone of negativity—associated with the dance, the people, and their culture—is swiftly established. There is little question, at least from the point of view of mid-1940s Hollywood, that such indigenous dance forms are savage, sinister, and sinful. Consequently, no effort is made to give any attention to the content or the quality of the dance.

In *Tarzan*, as in many similar films, the exact cultural context is difficult to discern. What defines the cultural ambiance is a cluster of sinister symbols, many of which are associated with the dance. The leopard is one such recurring element or symbol. Like both the dance and the culture as a whole, the leopard is seen as wild, dangerous, untamed. The snake is another familiar element in this context. These symbols reappear in *Live and Let Die* (1973), a film in the James Bond series which contains a *vodoun* ceremony staged by the Jamaican-born Geoffrey Holder. Here, the snake and the leopard are coupled with visions of death, skeletal images, and frightening masks. The actions of the dance embody brutal sexual overtones. *Vodoun* rituals are culturally specific to Haiti, parts of the Caribbean, and beyond, but in Hollywood's eyes, they could stand for virtually any indigenous religious ceremony. No wonder they have been a favorite Hollywood pretext for insensitive distortions.

Looking for more "primitive" patterns, I discovered similar material in three separate versions of *King Solomon's Mines*, produced from 1937 to 1985. This trio of films, based on the adventure novel by H. Rider Haggard, aptly demonstrates filmmakers' inconsistency in depicting cultural reality. The essence of Haggard's story—the saga of a white man looking for his brother, or a white woman looking for her husband or father—remains constant, and each of the three versions was at least partially shot on location in Africa. But the similarities end there.

Watusi warrior dance from "King Solomon's Mines," 1950,
courtesy Turner Entertainment Co.

One might reasonably expect Hollywood's awareness of cultural values to become more sophisticated over time, but any notion of historical progress is seriously challenged by this series of films. In the most recent version, produced by Golan-Globus in 1985 with Richard Chamberlain and Sharon Stone, we see the cluster of "primitive symbols" used to their fullest. This time they revolve around the "Leopard Woman," the principal ritualist in a climactic segment of the film. This sequence, a clear manipulation of quasi–East African elements, restates negative opinions of both dance and culture by focusing our attention on the same symbols and suggesting the same values as the early Tarzan films.

While the cultural context is absurdly manipulated in the 1985 *King Solomon's Mines*, it is nevertheless identifiable. The credits, for example, acknowledge the government and people of Zimbabwe. The earliest version, a British production shot in southeast Africa in 1937, is more sensitive to its surroundings, offering a traditional dance free of manipulations. But this sympathetic attitude is most fully revealed in MGM's 1950 production, in which we see the fairly accurate, ethnographically acceptable, culturally consistent presentation of a dance of Watusi warriors before their king. The integrity of the event is maintained as it is filmed in its appropriate location with actual Watusi warriors. Baziga of the Watusi tribe, a leading dancer in the sequence, is given a main credit on the film. A fine example of visual anthropology, the film records a sight no longer available to be seen because of the political desecration of this area of Africa. Thus, the 1950 *King Solomon's Mines* serves as an important document as well as being a pleasure to behold, and for this we must thank Hollywood.

NATIVE AMERICA

Meanwhile, the overall attitude toward Native American material has shifted enormously as the Hollywood "talkie" has evolved, and progress is apparent. In its treatment of both dance and other cultural issues, Hollywood has gone from being romantic and patronizing (and romanticism is often patronizing) to steadily sharpening its insights into Native American culture. This change in point of view is almost certainly the result of the pressure brought to bear by Native Americans on their own behalf, including direct lobbying by activists. With the coming of "Red Power" in the early 1970s it was no longer possible for filmmakers to get away with casting Native American cultures consistently as the Other. As a result, portrayals of these dances have improved.

One example of a peculiarly romantic early interpretation of Native American cultures is found in the film *Rose Marie* (1936), a vehicle for Nelson Eddy and Jeanette MacDonald, based on the Broadway hit. A central dance sequence includes a dizzying mixture of cultural references from Plains, Pueblo, and Northwest Coast tribes as well as something approximating the Deer Dance of the Yaqui tribe. While the Northwest is the purported locale of the story, the artifacts and costumes suggest not only totem poles of the Northwest but corn maidens and an Eagle Dancer of the Southwest Pueblos. A centerpiece of the dance is an enormous twelve-foot Plains big drum. Moreover, through the intentional alteration of the speed at which the film is shot, the filmmakers seem determined to avoid the perceived monotony of many traditional Native American forms and rhythms, establishing an almost jazzlike beat. The music, added after the filming, is played by a full European-style orchestra. The Totem Pole Dance was staged by Chester Hale, who was prominent in the mid-1930s for such ethnic sequences. He was also responsible for the Chinese ritual dance sequence in *The Painted Veil* (1934), which evidenced this same romanticized, hybrid interpretation.

While some cowboy-and-Indian films used brief flashes of "war dances" to establish the barbarity of the Indians, those scenes that focus on the dance itself reveal an even more patronizing attitude. For example, in a sequence from *Susannah of the Mounties* (1939), Shirley Temple plays the daughter of a captain in the Mounted Police who is attempting to learn a dance sequence from her playmate, a Blackfoot Indian. She moves in the crouching stomp so often imitated as Native American dance movement and puts her hand to her mouth, singing "Wa, wa, wa." Perhaps unconsciously embarrassed by the ridiculous parody, she bursts into laughter. "No more dancing. Squaw laugh," says the young Blackfoot. Temple replies, "I'm awfully sorry, honest. I won't do it anymore." Her mother, dressed in formal evening attire, attempts to make amends. "We're enjoying it," she says. "Please don't stop. Perhaps one day you will teach me an Indian dance." Note the "benevolent white father" tone of this conversation and the subtext that dance is only an entertainment. Ironically, Temple often played the innocent chameleon of dance, whether in her accomplished performance of hula in *Captain January* (1936) or her buck-and-wing with African-American dancer Bill Robinson in *The Little Colonel* (1935).

This dance-as-commodity attitude had already altered somewhat with the release of *Valley of the Sun* (1942), a melodrama that attempted to be more sympathetic to the Native American point of view. The protagonist (actor James Craig) is a white man who has aligned himself with the Indians, and the film's dramatic tension is created by his speaking on behalf of the Indians to his fellow white men. In line with that theme, this film gives more serious attention to the dance. We see brief portions of Fancy Dances, an important element of any pan–Indian powwow; a Grass Dance; and a Hoop Dance. These are performed in a traditional manner by traditional performers and the film's credits acknowledge the participation of members of the Pueblos of Taos, Santa Clara, Jemez, San Juan, and Tesuque in New Mexico.

Lucille Ball and James Craig with Hoop Dancers in "Valley of the Sun," 1942, courtesy Turner Entertainment Co.

The film's dialogue also attempts to develop some understanding of the cultural functions of dance. The hero explains to Lucille Ball, the young heroine, that the role of these dances is analogous to the "rice and old shoes" in Western wedding traditions. Despite serious flaws in this interpretation, there is, in the scripting, an attempt to understand the function of dance that distinguishes it from *Susannah of the Mounties*. This is one of the first such attempts. A *Man Called Horse* (1970) goes much further. The last quarter of the film is an elaborate yet thoughtful recreation of portions of the Sun Dance as practiced by members of the Rosebud Sioux Tribe, who appear in the film. With A *Man Called Horse* we sense Hollywood's attempt to present a Native American point of view, a point of view greatly expanded in the recent *Dances With Wolves* (1990).

THE PACIFIC ISLANDS

A decidedly paternalistic attitude pervades Hollywood's reconstruction of Pacific Island cultures and dance, where dance is almost always presented in the context of a feast or a luau. The situation in general is one of conviviality, although a sinister overtheme sometimes intrudes. The white man is seen as capable of manipulating these naïve, childlike Pacific Islanders who, like children at play, go on doing their own thing in their own way. The dance is the hula, which is repeated over and over in various forms with varying themes, while the occasional male Knife Dance is thrown in for contrast. When, in *Song of the Islands* (1942), Betty Grable performs her version of this dance on a fictional Hawaiian island, the lyrics she sings to the islanders reveal the prevailing Hollywood attitude:

> You have never heard of Jello
> Or of Abbott and Costello
> Or that Alka-Seltzer helps you for a while.
> You don't know just who Professor Quiz is
> On Ami Ami Oni Oni Isle.

In the opening sequence of *Honolulu*, Eleanor Powell comments on a dance she and George Brent are viewing. "It is lovely, George," she says, "which hula is it?" Brent replies, "Oh, it was just a hula." Eleanor is affronted: "But what does it mean? Do you mean to tell me, after living in the islands for so long, you don't realize that the hula tells a story?"

After that astute comment by Powell, we move into a sequence that ends with her well-known "tap dance hula" to island rhythms. (What story is that telling, Eleanor?) There are a number of such bizarre interpretations by Caucasian leading ladies—all apparently just "in fun."

As we so often discover, Hollywood sees what it wants to see and understands what it wants to understand. The sexual overtones of the hula, with its moving hips, for instance, are systematically overemphasized to the exclusion of subtler characteristics. This is a theme that runs throughout the Pacific Island films. At another point in Grable's "Ami Ami Oni Oni Isle" song, she sings:

> When you're underneath the banyan
> With a beautiful companion
> Close your eyes and dream it up a little while.
> Open them and if you are in heaven,
> It's Ami Ami Oni Oni Isle.

A sequence from *Pagan Love Song* (1950) points out still more complex reverberations of Hollywood's interaction with Hawaiian culture. These dances are excellent examples of what Adrienne Kaeppler would call "airport art," adaptations made by the islanders specifically for the tourist *haole*, a Hawaiian word that translates roughly as "white person" or "foreigner."[2] This is the kind of performance often presented in a hotel or nightclub setting and it is in this context that the dance sequences appear in the film.

---

2. "Polynesian Dance as 'Airport Art,'" in Adrienne Kaeppler, Judy Van Zile, and Carl Wolz, eds., *Asian and Pacific Dance* (*Dance Research Annual*) (Congress on Research in Dance, 1977), pp. 71–84.

Approaching the topic from a Hawaiian point of view, however, we might understand "airport art" as an internally generated transformation of cultural forms, already influenced by
Hollywood. In this way, the Other conforms cultural expression to the perceived worldview and preferences of the *haole*. In
Pagan Love Song, for example, Western values are already incor-
porated into the dance and the Western "cover girl" bias against
larger women is also present. In Pacific cultures, weight and
size are a mark of pride and prestige, but these attributes are
only treated comically by Hollywood. In most Pacific Island
films, for instance, there is a fat, jolly woman who is the chief
clown and merry-maker, for example, the Hilo Hattie character
in *Song of the Islands*.

ASIA

Hollywood's prevailing perception of Asia is that of an amalgam of cultures. Any film purporting to be located in an Asian
country is likely to include visual elements from other areas as
well, mixing cultural symbols from China, Japan, Indochina,
Indonesia, and India. Cultural specificity is largely lacking in
these Hollywood treatments. Instead, elements are mixed together and presented as a fantasy or a fairy tale. These visual-
izations are also usually highly theatrical. The audience is
meant to be fascinated by the context—mesmerized, en-
chanted, perhaps seduced. We find such fusions in dance
sequences from motion pictures as different as *Painted Veil*
(1934) and *Road to Bali* (1952). Two wonderfully romanticized
processionals from *Kismet* (1955), set in Baghdad and choreographed by Jack Cole, provide a fine example of "oriental"
conglomeration. We note all the elements essential to ritual
dance-dramas throughout Asia—the banners, the umbrellas,
the offering of flowers and foodstuffs—but the result is still a
hybrid, an imaginative potpourri that is marvelously fantastic
and fairy tale-like. What is clear on viewing these films is that

"The Small House of Uncle Thomas" from "The King and I," 1956,
© Twentieth Century Fox Film Corporation

they were not produced by individuals who were concerned with Asian cultures for their own integrity and reality. No wonder the dance sequences presented in these films suffer.

Even in "The Small House of Uncle Thomas" from *The King and I* (1956), adapted by Jerome Robbins from his Broadway show choreography, fantasy elements are combined in a surprising amalgam. The wonderfully imaginative and visually exciting rainstorm in the opening portion of the dance derives from Japanese Noh theater rather than Thai dance-drama traditions. Overall, however, this piece is quite different from previous examples I have given because it does demonstrate a sensitive understanding of Thai dance and Thai culture. The integrity possible in fusions is nowhere better demonstrated than in the imaginative "How to Walk on Frozen Water" section. The skating movements of Eliza and the angel as they cross the frozen river reflect an experience with which most Americans, but few Thais, are familiar. At the same time, the style of this sequence is completely in keeping with the Thai classical movement alphabet and underlines the theme addressed in the performance as a whole. This is a linkage of understandings that does not negate cultural values.

The complexities Robbins faced in choreographing "Small House" were enormous, the perceptual filters multilayered: an American theatrical representation of a Thai (Siamese) interpretation of an American classic—Uncle Tom's Cabin. Packed with its own racial issues, the tale is placed furthermore in the context of a story about cultural confrontations. "The Small House of Uncle Thomas" sequence takes from and interprets an Asian culture with respect and concern; yet we begin to see something else in Robbins' modus operandi. In evaluating this piece we are led to talk not about bias and prejudice but rather Robbins' masterly creation of a new aesthetic.

In a different way, we find a new aesthetic emerging in other Hollywood interpretations of Asian forms. The dance sequences from Road to Bali, for example, are very jazzlike, which raises the interesting question of how much influence Jack Cole, the choreographer, had on a general Hollywood fusion and confusion between Asian movement vocabulary—with its detailing of gesture and posture—and jazz, particularly since Cole's Hollywood jazz style continued to be influenced by the "oriental" dance to which he had been introduced by Ruth St. Denis and Ted Shawn. This too might be considered an example of a new aesthetic, a cultural distortion transformed into a new entity.

In recent years, another shift has taken place, similar to that which occurred in films representing the Native American experience. In Karate Kid II (1986), for example, we find an honest representation and contextualization of an O Bon celebration in an Okinawan community. This film demonstrates an aware and sympathetic attitude toward dance. Since it is, in part, addressed to the Japanese-American community, the film begins to reflect a cultural insider's viewpoint. Because the people who are affected by these interpretations are directly available, the producer and director are forced to be cognizant of their concerns.

SOUTH AMERICA

Quite a different point of view is evident in Hollywood's treatment of South America and its dance forms. By contrast, the attitude toward dance is positive, persuasive, and embracing. The interpretation favored by most directors and choreographers is that rhythm permeates these cultures and that one is drawn into the culture by participating in the dance. In *Down Argentine Way* (1940), Betty Grable is caught in a swirl of rumbas and tangos. In *Fire Down Below* (1957), choreographed by Tutte Lemkow, there is a powerful sequence in which Rita Hayworth is virtually sucked into and carried away by the dance.

Likewise, *They Met in Argentina* (1941), richly choreographed by Frank Veloz of the ballroom team of Veloz and Yolanda,

"Down Argentine Way," 1940,
© *Twentieth Century Fox Film Corporation*

treats the dance with a kind of honor and attention that is often absent from movie choreographers' approaches to the dances of other cultural and geographic areas. The film ends with the request, "Now, everybody, join in the dance," focusing our attention not on performance but participation. What we are seeing and experiencing encourages us to be swept away, to throw ourselves into a culture that has such a positive attitude toward dance.

Even in cartoons, dance is depicted as the heartbeat, the pulse of South American cultures. A sequence from Walt Disney's *Three Caballeros* (1945) epitomizes this experience: everything—the lamp posts, the buildings, the city—vibrates with the rhythms of Brazil. On the other hand, it should also be noted that the sources of these rhythms (African and indigenous South and Central American cultures) are not even obliquely addressed.

Hollywood bias, in other words, can cut two ways. It can be very negative or it can be overly positive. In either case, Hollywood fails to deal with reality. In the case of South America, some of the problems existing in these societies are glossed over by the fantasy that all is beautiful, all is dance, all is rhythm.

In sharp contrast to these fantasies about South America are two last films, *Tango Bar* (1988) and *Black Orpheus* (1958), which were distributed through Hollywood channels but which were made in Central or South America. Their richness derives from the fact that they are very much involved with reality.

A coproduction of Puerto Rican and Argentinian producers, *Tango Bar* is concerned with the cultural attitude of Buenos Aires in the late 1970s to early 1980s—those years of horror during which Argentina was ruled by a military *junta*. The film examines the concept of tango, both the music and dance, in the context of the political dynamics in that country. The tango is described as the heart of the barrio, shaped by men "with persistence and courage." It is also called "that sad thought made into dance." The political situation is examined through the personae of two musicians, Ricardo and Antonio, who perform as a successful nightclub duo. The story concerns the separate paths they take, with the pianist Ricardo continuing to live in Buenos Aires under dictatorship while Antonio, who plays the bandoneon, moves away from that center of Argentinian culture into the larger world, taking with him tango music and dance. The issue of censorship is addressed in the story line of the film. Antonio senses that art itself is in the process of being compromised and attacked. The *junta* has censored the tango, and Antonio is concerned that soon they will be dictating what to sing, too. Ricardo on the other hand is of the opinion that leaving Buenos Aires is betraying the country: "You lose the language, the scent of the city." Years later, after the dictatorship has been overthrown, Ricardo and Antonio are brought together again by the tango.

In a reflexive turn, *Tango Bar* also reviews the tango in the context of Hollywood, whose misunderstanding of the form is pointedly demonstrated by several interpretations of "La Cumparsita," the most popular and overused tango in the United States. *Tango Bar* shows both the distortions perpetrated on the dance because of the American interest in this particular style and the overlapping of Latin-American forms. It gives some wonderful examples of "La Cumparsita" as danced by Rudolph Valentino, the Flintstones, Charlie Chaplin, Laurel and Hardy, and Gene Kelly. To quote *Tango Bar* itself, Hollywood lent the tango "luxury, excess, grandeur, acrobatics."

Black Orpheus, made by Brazilian, Italian, and French producers, is also political in its overall impact, placing the socializing and organizing dynamic of Carnival in Rio in the context of a community of poverty. What these films suggest is that while the pervading Hollywood attitude about dance in the Americas is generally supportive, we are most sensitized to the functions of dance when we see through the eyes of the members of these cultures themselves.

Hollywood images of world dance are both powerful and provocative and allow many potential interpretations. Some blatantly insensitive distortions concerning dance and culture were presented by Hollywood through the late 1940s—a time when dance tended to be viewed and used as an artifact completely separable from culture. Considered generic in function as well as form, dance was often seen as the very thing that made "primitive" people "primitive." This point of view is less common today, though it is far from extinct.

Even though Hollywood has sometimes engaged in distortion, both of dance forms and cultural contexts, its approach to world dance has also transformed such distortion into new entities and made an impact on indigenous forms. "Airport art," for example, which is perhaps most prevalent in Pacific Island cultures, includes dances done by islanders themselves, incorporating their own choreographic changes and manipulations. These changes are internally generated transformations of cultural forms that were heavily influenced by Hollywood. Such new forms evolved because the people from within the culture sought ways to conform to the American tourist's expectations, expectations that were most clearly articulated in the Hollywood worldview.

In other instances the amalgamation and conglomeration of cultures and the mixing together of indigenous and "Hollywood" elements—such as has often occurred with Asia-based material—have led to "fusion" and the creation of new genres. Possible in these fusions is a linkage of understandings that does not negate cultural values but rather evolves into a new aesthetic. We see this in the magnificent work of Jerome Robbins in "The Small House of Uncle Thomas" where, through a sensitive understanding of Thai dance and Thai culture, a fresh and very contemporary statement emerges. Jack Cole's Hollywood jazz genre, a new and original vocabulary, is another example of a new aesthetic that evolved from the fusion of forms.

As filmmakers become more sensitive to cultural context, choreographed movement may actually disappear, as will the choreographer in his/her current role, while the role of ethnologist-choreographer will emerge. At the same time, the filmic approach may become more documentary than creative. The Watusi sequence from the 1950 version of *King Solomon's Mines* is an early example of what could become a strong trend in the 1990s. The dances documented in more recent films concerned with Native American experience—particularly the 1970 *A Man Called Horse*, made with the cooperation of the Rosebud Sioux Tribe, and the 1990 *Dances With Wolves*—are other important examples. Such marvelously inviting and participatory experiences as those created by films like *Tango Bar* and *Black Orpheus* also demonstrate that we are most sensitized to dance and culture when the "feel" of dance and the understanding of the culture from which it springs are provided by members of the subject cultures themselves.

With some nostalgia, I remember the old Fox Movietone slogan which called film "the eyes and the ears of the world." Let us add to that the dancing body. Through film, the world vision—shown to us through the eyes of members of world cultures—is more readily available, more capable of enriching our perceptual abilities than ever before. Increasingly, we recognize that each country's own dreams should become its reality and that the people themselves should have the right to speak out and represent themselves in film and video. Hollywood, as a single monolithic perspective, no longer holds total power, although it has contributed tremendously in our lives to the way we see the world—and to the way the world sees itself.

FILMS CITED

Black Orpheus, 1958, Lopert Films; producer: Sasha Gordine; director: Marcel Camus; stars: Breno Mello, Marpessa Dawn.

Captain January, 1936, Twentieth Century Fox; producer: Darryl F. Zanuck; director: David Butler; stars: Shirley Temple, Guy Kibbee, Buddy Ebsen.

Dances With Wolves, 1990, Orion Pictures; producer: TIG Productions, Kevin Costner, Jim Wilson; director: Kevin Costner; stars: Kevin Costner, Mary McDonnell, Graham Greene, Rodney A. Grant.

Down Argentine Way, 1940, Twentieth Century Fox; producer: Darryl F. Zanuck; director: Irving Cummings; stars: Don Ameche, Betty Grable (dancer), Carmen Miranda; dances staged by Nicholas Castle, Geneva Sawyer.

Fire Down Below, 1957, Columbia/Warwick; producers: Irving Allen, Albert R. Broccoli; director: Robert Parrish; stars: Rita Hayworth (dancer), Robert Mitchum, Jack Lemmon; choreography: Tutte Lemkow; "Limbo Dance" by the "Stretch" Cox Troupe.

Honolulu, 1939, MGM; producer: Jack Cummings; director: Edward Buzzell; stars: Eleanor Powell (dancer), Robert Young, Kealoha Holt (native dancing girl); dances by Bobby Connelly, Sammy Lee.

The Karate Kid II, 1986, Columbia Pictures; producer: Jerry Weintraub; director: John G. Avildsen; stars: Ralph Macchio, Noriyuki "Pat" Morita, Tamlyn Tomita.

The King and I, 1956, Twentieth Century Fox; producer: Charles Brackett; director: Walter Lang; stars: Deborah Kerr, Yul Brynner, Rita Moreno; dances and musical numbers staged by Jerome Robbins; consultant on oriental dance: Michiko.

King Solomon's Mines, 1937, Gaumont British Picture Corp. Ltd.; producer: Geoffrey Barkas; director: Robert Stevenson; African exteriors directed by Geoffrey Barkas; stars: Paul Robeson, Cedric Hardwicke, Roland Young.

King Solomon's Mines, 1950, MGM; producer: Sam Zimbalist; directors: Compton Bennett, Andrew Marton; stars: Deborah Kerr, Stewart Granger, Richard Carlson, Kimursi of the Kipsigi Tribe, Sirague, Seraryongo, Baziga of the Watusi Tribe. End credit states that MGM is grateful to the government officials of Tanganyika, Uganda Protectorate, Kenya Colony and Protectorate, Belgian Congo.

King Solomon's Mines, 1985, Golan-Globus Productions; producers: Menahem Golan, Yoram Globus; director: J. Lee Thompson; stars: Richard Chamberlain, Sharon Stone, Herbert Lom. End credit includes the producers' thanks to the Government and People of Zimbabwe.

Kismet, 1955, MGM; producer: Arthur Freed; director: Vincente Minnelli; stars: Howard Keel, Ann Blyth; musical numbers and dances staged by Jack Cole.

The Little Colonel, 1935, Twentieth Century Fox; producer: B. G. DeSylva; director: David Butler; stars: Shirley Temple, Lionel Barrymore.

Live and Let Die, 1973, United Artists; producers: Albert R. Broccoli, Harry Saltzman; director: Guy Hamilton; stars: Roger Moore, Yaphet Kotto, Jane Seymour; choreographer: Geoffrey Holder.

A Man Called Horse, 1970, Sanford Howard Productions Corp.; producer: Sanford Howard; director: Elliot Silverstein; stars: Richard Harris, Iron Eyes Cody, members of the Rosebud Sioux Tribe.

Pagan Love Song, 1950, MGM; producer: Arthur Freed; director: Robert Alton; stars: Esther Williams, Howard Keel.

The Painted Veil, 1934, MGM; producer: Hunt Stromberg; director: Richard Boleslawski; stars: Greta Garbo, George Brent; "Chinese Fantasy" conceived by Hubert Stowitts, staged by Chester Hale.

Pardon My Sarong, 1942, Universal; producer: Alex Gottlieb; director: Erle C. Kenton; stars: Lou Costello, Bud Abbott, Lionel Atwill, Virginia Prince; dances staged by Katherine Dunham with dancers Tip, Tap, and Toc and the Katherine Dunham Dancers.

Rhythm of the Islands, 1943, Universal; producer: Bernard Burton; director: Roy William Neill; stars: Allan Jones, Jane Frazee; choreography: Lester Horton.

Road to Bali, 1952, Paramount; producer: Harry Tugend; director: Hal Walker; stars: Bing Crosby, Bob Hope, Dorothy Lamour; musical numbers by Charles O'Curran.

Rose Marie, 1936, MGM; producer: Hunt Stromberg; director: W.S. Van Dyke; stars: Jeanette MacDonald, Nelson Eddy; "Totem Pole Dance" staged by Chester Hale.

Song of the Islands, 1942, Twentieth Century Fox; producer: William Le Baron; director: Walter Lang; stars: Betty Grable (dancer), Victor Mature, Jack Oakie, Hilo Hattie (dancer); dances staged by Hermes Pan.

Susannah of the Mounties, 1939, Twentieth Century Fox; associate producer: Kenneth MacGowan; director: William A. Seiter; stars: Shirley Temple, Randolph Scott, Margaret Lockwood, members of the Blackfoot Reservation of Montana.

Tango Bar, 1988, Beco Films/Zaga Films; producers: Roberto Gandava and Juan Carlos Codazzi; director: Marios Zurinaga; stars: Raul Julia, Valeria Lynch, Ruben Juarez.

Tarzan and the Leopard Woman, 1946, RKO; associate producer and director: Kurt Neumann; stars: Johnny Weissmuller, Brenda Joyce, Johnny Sheffield; dance director: Lester Horton.

They Met in Argentina, 1941, RKO; producer: Lou Brock; director: Leslie Goodwins, Jack Hively; stars: Maureen O'Hara, James Ellison, Buddy Ebsen (dancer); dance director: Frank Veloz.

The Three Caballeros, 1945, Walt Disney; production supervisor and director: Norman Ferguson; stars: José Carioca, Donald Duck; choreography: Billy Daniels, Aloysio Oliveira, Carmelita Maracci.

Valley of the Sun, 1942, RKO; producer: Graham Baker; director: George Marshall; stars: Lucille Ball, James Craig, Dean Jagger, Indians from the Pueblos of Taos, Santa Clara, Jemez, San Juan, and Tesuque.

STRIPPING THE EMPEROR

Brenda Dixon Gottschild

Several years ago, a student in my course at Temple University titled "Black Performance from Africa to the Americas" came up to me at the end of the first session and asked, "Should I take this class ... I mean, as a white person?" The question animated her face with confusion and fear. My response was, "Honey, you're taking it right now; you've been taking it all your life!" As Americans, we are all "enrolled" in this course. Some of us do not know it; some do, but deny it. For Americans, the Africanist legacy is not a choice but an imperative that comes to us through the culture.[1]

Unlike the voluntary taking on of Easternisms in modern and postmodern practice, the Africanist legacy comes to Americans as electricity comes through the wires: we draw from it all the time, but few of us are aware of its sources. To quote Toni Morrison, it is "the ghost in the machine" or "the unspeakable things unspoken."[2] It infuses our daily existence in musical forms such as blues, jazz, spirituals, gospel, soul, rap, funk,

Temple University and the Pennsylvania Council on the Arts provided partial support for this ongoing research project.

1. The term "Africanist" is used here to include diasporan concepts, practices, attitudes, or forms which have roots or origins in Africa. ("Diaspora" refers to the dispersion of African peoples from their homeland, beginning in the transatlantic slave trade era.) My precedent for using this term is set in recent scholarship. For example, see Joseph E. Holloway, *Africanisms in American Culture* (Bloomington: Indiana University Press, 1990) and Toni Morrison, *Playing in the Dark: Whiteness and the Literary Imagination* (Cambridge, Mass.: Harvard University Press, 1992).
2. "Unspeakable Things Unspoken: The Afro-American Presence in American Literature," *Michigan Quarterly Review* (Winter 1989), 11.

◀ *George Balanchine and Katherine Dunham rehearsing "Cabin in the Sky,"* 1940, *photo by* W. Eugene Smith, © The Heirs of W. Eugene Smith, *courtesy The Center for Creative Photography, University of Arizona* rock, and yes, even European orchestral music. It is a considerable force in modern American arts and letters, as has been discussed by Morrison and other literary critics. It permeates American dance forms, from ballroom and nightclub floors to popular and concert stages. Finally, it pervades our everyday lifestyles, in ways of walking, talking, creating hairdos, preparing food, and acting "hip" or "cool."

But there is a problem: the Africanist aesthetic, though readily apparent in American culture, is rarely acknowledged. Morrison's "unspeakable things unspoken" describes the territory assigned to Africanisms in American culture because what is spoken or silenced depends on who is speaking. Who is doing the documenting? From whose perspective? By whose criteria? And what is being recorded? The act of *naming* is an assertion of power. That which is unnamed or misnamed remains mute, inconsequential, and insignificant.

There are at least two principal American cultures: African and European, fused but also separate. Due to discrimination and segregation, cultural misunderstanding has become our normal mode of cultural exchange. As Americans, one way we could learn to embrace our conflicts is to reverse positions and see American culture as Africanist and look at the European elements in a different light. Such a revisionist perspective is the basis of my exposition of American concert dance; of dance ethnologist Joann Kealiinohomoku's signature essay, "An Anthropologist Looks at Ballet as a Form of Ethnic Dance"; and of Toni Morrison's *Playing in the Dark: Whiteness and the Literary Imagination*.[3] Duke University historian Peter Wood suggested to the planners of Colonial Williamsburg that, in reconstructing that site, all roles be reversed, with African Americans depicting plantation owners and European Americans

---

3. Kealiinohomoku, *Impulse* (1969–1970), 24–33, reprinted in Roger Copeland and Marshall Cohen, eds., *What is Dance?* (New York: Oxford University Press, 1983), pp. 533–549; Morrison (1992), *op. cit.*

playing slaves.[4] That could have been a good learning experience for all involved, especially the spectators. But as anyone
might have guessed, the idea did not catch on.

The Africanist presence has existed in European-American
culture since plantation-era contacts between Africans and
Europeans, contacts that forged and shaped a unique,
creolized, Afro-Euro-American culture that all Americans embrace, consciously and subliminally, whether they admit it or
not. Its impact on us, as dance people and as Americans, can
be felt through many means besides dance.

Here are some cultural flashpoints.

There are many cases of African-inspired beauty standards
providing exotic fodder for mainstream consumption. Some
examples include the frizzy perm of the 1970s—in response to
the Afro of the 1960s—and media figures like Bo Derek adopt-
ing braided or dreadlocked coiffures. Hardly a game of com-
petitive sports is complete without the exchange on the field
of Africanist-inspired handslaps or hip/buttock/pelvic excla-
mation points. European-American pop musicians have
adopted the look, the sound, and the phrasing of the Africanist
aesthetic. Elvis Presley is only the most famous example of a
phenomenon so widespread that it is taken for granted, and
its roots, unfortunately, are unacknowledged.

European Americans down South grew up and lived their
lives with African Americans, and the Africanist legacy was
almost literally in the air they breathed. Others "arrived" through
music. One British writer characterized jazz as marrow in the
bones of European culture:

> We are so accustomed to hearing jazz and Ameri-
> can-influenced popular music—the sound of the
> 20th century—that our ears cannot imagine a world
> of sound without the freedom of syncopated jazz.[5]

4. Personal communication, 1988.
5. *London Observer Sunday Magazine* (19 January 1986), 20.

How telling a statement, and how true. Many of us are aware that popular American music is dominated by Africanist invention, but how many realize that concert music from Stravinsky and Milhaud to Glass and Reich is also infused with Africanisms?

Theater played a large part in the appropriation of the Africanist aesthetic. To break the stranglehold of mainstream theater, many experimental groups of the 1960s and thereafter looked not only to Eastern sources (which are well documented as avant-garde inspiration) but frequently to Africanisms as well. I was a member of The Open Theater, one of those pioneering groups. We used sources ranging from the cakewalk to Candomblé (an Afro-Brazilian religion) in our theatrical explorations. The most recent work of theater innovator Jerzy Grotowski, whose small team of collaborators is based in Pontedera, Italy, provides a useful 1990s example:

> There are few discernible words, but these rhythmic, highly structured vocal works—some derived from African and Caribbean initiation rites—have an uncanny resonance and vibration. . . . Their carefully controlled movements, based on ancient forms of concentration, include a special way of holding the spine and protruding the backside, much like the warrior's position in primordial tribes. The stance, silent and attentive, is supposed to energize and enliven the body and awaken a certain innate physical power and mindfulness.[6]

The vestiges of that stance, still discernible in the posture of contemporary peoples of African lineage, has been maligned in the ballet world and used as evidence to prove the inappropriateness of the African body for ballet.

---

6. Margaret Croyden, "Jerzy Grotowski—The Experiment Continues," *American Theatre* (September 1992), 42.

Here is an especially powerful flashpoint. The black civil rights movement of the 1950s and 1960s was the locus of origin for a nationwide revolutionary spirit and a desire for reorganization of political and social structures. It became the prototype for the subsequent women's, antiwar, and environmental protest movements, offering an immediate model for liberation. An alternative form of society could exist and even thrive within an alien superculture. Contact improvisation seems to have drawn unconsciously from the civil rights movement the inspiration and model for its own freedom of movement in dance—not in content, of course, but in attitude. In another example of inadvertent borrowing, even the contact improviser's "jam" takes its name from the jazz musician's "jam session." These jams see contactors from far and wide converge to hold a marathon, paralleling the traditional form of African-American revival meetings. In fact, our society is permeated by Africanist attitudes and forms, from the agrarian practices of Africa, which were basic to the success of plantation agriculture, to such Africanist specifics as potato chips, peanut butter, and the Charleston.

So much of what we see as avant-garde in the postmodern movement is actually informed by recycled Africanist principles. The coolness, relaxation, looseness, and laid-back energy; the radical juxtaposition of ostensibly contrary elements; the irony and double-entendre of verbal and physical gesture; the dialogic relationship of performer and audience—all are integral elements in Africanist arts and lifestyle, which are dreadlocked into the weave of our society and inherited by Americans, black and white. When Douglas Dunn quotes ballet without straight legs or heroic energy, or Yvonne Rainer creates a solo, titles it a trio (Trio A), and bases it on movement clusters and an indirect approach to the audience, they redefine their idiom. They may not be aware that the Africanist aesthetic is nonlinear and values dance steps that are dense, self-referential, and choreographed in clumps or clusters. (This approach to dancemaking, from a Eurocentric perspective, has been regarded as "cluttered" or "bad.") They probably do know that in hip talk "that's bad" means "that's good," and "that's down" means "that's up." Irony, paradox, and double-entendre, rather than the classical European linear logic of cause, effect, and resolution, are basic to the Africanist aesthetic and offer a model for postmodernism, subconsciously as well as cognitively.

Others were touched by the Africanist presence as they reached out for the dangerous, the illicit, the hip, the *primitive*. The "seduction of the primitive" is a trope that has played havoc with the European psyche since the Age of Enlightenment. It is a love-hate relationship of binary opposites, with the black (dancing) body as the screen upon which Europeans projected their fears and phobias along with their fantasies and desires. It is the primitive trope that defines the European concept of the Other, be it the *Hottentot Venus* in nineteenth-century London, Josephine Baker in twentieth-century Paris, "Ashanti Fever" in turn-of-the-century Vienna, or the consciously non-European influences in the revolutionary work of artists such as Picasso, Braque, and Matisse.[7]

It is a well-documented fact that Picasso's art took a different course after his exposure to African sculpture. In his trailblazing work, *Les Demoiselles d'Avignon*, two figures were influenced by African masks. The pictorial plane was broken into angular wedges. The style was termed Cubism. What if it had been called Africanism? Such a choice might have helped to advance understanding of the Africanist legacy in modernism

7. For a full discussion of the primitive trope in various settings and perspectives, see the following sources: Marianna Torgovnick, *Gone Primitive: Savage Intellects, Modern Lives* (Chicago: University of Chicago Press, 1990); Henry Louis Gates, *"Race," Writing, and Difference* (Chicago: University of Chicago Press, 1985); Sally Price, *Primitive Art in Civilized Places* (Chicago: University of Chicago Press, 1989); and Reinhold Grimm and Jost Hermand, eds., *Blacks and German Culture* (Madison: University of Wisconsin Press, 1986).

and the place of African peoples living in non-African societies. There are innumerable examples of Africanisms in modern art, in the work of artists such as Picasso, Braque, Leger, Matisse, Modigliani, Lipschitz, right up through Jackson Pollock. As in contact improvisation, Pollock's work is Africanist not in content but in attitude. A serious jazz enthusiast, Pollock was known to paint while listening to jazz music and, like the traditional African artist designing patterns on fabric, worked with his canvas on the floor, transforming the act of painting into a movement process involving the whole body. Like the jazz musician, he worked directly with improvisation.[8]

Likewise, there are many examples of the primitive as a major trope in modern dance. According to dance pundit Louis Horst, "Primitive art is evident as a strong quality in every contemporary style."[9] In his book *Modern Dance Forms*, he compares modern dance poses by artists such as Martha Graham with African statuary and modern art paintings. He contends that most modern dance is "primitive to a degree," and that some have totally borrowed the primitive mold. In 1930, in an article entitled "Seeking an American Art of the Dance," Martha Graham said, "We have two primitive sources, dangerous and hard to handle in the arts, but of intense psychic significance—the Indian and the Negro. That these influence us is certain."[10] This significant acknowledgment by the grande dame of modern dance has gone unnoticed. It simply fell through an interstice in history, as has the acknowledgment of those influences.

In Horst's chapter on jazz dance, he attributes its beginnings to enslaved Africans and then states, "It [jazz] does not imitate the typical ethnic African, but it retains many of the

8. See Andrew Kagan, "Improvisations: Notes on Jackson Pollock and the Black Contribution to American High Culture," *Arts* 53 (March 1979), 96–99.
9. Horst, *Modern Dance Forms* (Pennington, New Jersey: Princeton Book Company, 1987; first published,1961), p. 53.
10. Quoted in Juana de Laban, "What Tomorrow?" *Dance Observer* (May 1945), 55.

attributes brought from Africa." Among these he lists "jerky, percussive movements and accents," "syncopation," and "melancholy and lassitude."[11] He then goes on to mention the pervasive, subliminal influence of jazz in America:

> Although jazz is by now cosmopolitan and international, and has proved its affinity to the whole modern world by its popularity with all races and cultures, still it is most typically American. It is natural to all Americans, as deeply and subconsciously understood as any other folk dance is understood by the people from whom it grew. It is specifically the expression of present-day urban America. It is an intimate part of our daily life and shows in the urban walk, the posture, the rhythm of speech, the gesture, the costumes, of the city. It belongs to a certain way we have of standing—a slouch, one hip thrown out—of sitting in an informal sprawl, of speaking in slangy abruptness. Jazz is the trade mark of the city.[12]

The jazz characteristics described by Horst are Africanisms that infuse every aspect of American endeavor and can be summed up by the phrase, "aesthetic of the cool."

What Africanisms am I talking about? They emerge from aesthetic principles, or canons, that have been codified and discussed at length by other authors, particularly Robert Farris Thompson, Susan Vogel, Kariamu Welsh Asante, and to a lesser extent, Geneva Gay and Will L. Baber, and Alfred Pasteur and Ivory Toldson.[13] From these sources I have designated five

---

11. Horst (1987/1961), p. 111.
12. Ibid., pp. 111–112.
13. For a thorough discussion that is applicable to both visual and performing arts, see Thompson, *African Art in Motion* (Los Angeles: University of California Press, 1974). Thompson compiles an Africanist aesthetic paradigm that he terms

Africanist characteristics that occur in many forms of American concert dance, including ballet. It is important to note that these traits work together and are separated only for the sake of discussion. They indicate processes, tendencies, and attitudes. They are not intended to categorize phenomena. To show their interactive nature, I use the dance routine of Earl "Snake Hips" Tucker to illustrate each canon. An African-American novelty dancer who attained enormous popularity in the cabarets of the 1920s, Tucker makes these Africanist principles clearly visible in his work. Ballet, the academic dance of Europe, offers the most dramatic contrast to the Africanist aesthetic. It has been regarded as the repository of European values and is characterized as a reflection of "what is thought most significant in the culture of the West."[14] For these reasons, I use ballet, rather than European vernacular dance, as the European reference point in the five principles that follow.

EMBRACING THE CONFLICT

In a broad sense, the Africanist aesthetic can be termed an aesthetic of contrariety, while the European perspective seeks to remove conflict through efficient problem solving. The Africanist aesthetic embraces difference and dissonance, rather than erasing or resolving it. Contrariety is expressed in African dilemma stories that pose a question rather than offer a solution; in music or vocal work that sounds cacophonous or grating to the untrained ear; and in dance that seems unsophisticated to eyes trained in a different aesthetic. This

the "Ten Canons of Fine Form." See also Vogel, *Aesthetics of African Art* (New York: Center for African Art, 1986) and Asante, "Commonalities in African Dance," in *African Culture—The Rhythms of Unity,* Molefi Kete Asante and Kariamu Welsh Asante, eds. (Westport: Greenwood Press, 1986), pp. 71–82, for a dance-specific discussion of Africanist aesthetics. For a more generalized discussion of Africanisms in America, see also Gay and Baber, eds., *Expressively Black: The Cultivated Basis of Ethnic Identity* (New York: Praeger, 1987) and Pasteur and Toldson, *Roots of Soul: The Psychology of Black Expressiveness* (New York: Anchor, 1982).

14. Rayner Heppenstall, quoted in Selma Jeanne Cohen, *Next Week, Swan Lake* (Middletown, Conn.: Wesleyan University Press, 1982), p. 131.

principle is reflected in the other four canons and they, in turn, are reflected in it. "Embracing the conflict" is embedded in the final principle, "the aesthetic of the cool," in which "coolness" results from the juxtaposition of detachment and intensity. Those opposites would be difficult to fuse in European

Earl "Snake Hips" Tucker, 1928, courtesy Frank Driggs Collection

academic aesthetics, but there is room for their pairing in Africanist aesthetics. A routine performed by Tucker in such New York clubs as Connie's Inn and Harlem's Cotton Club—as described in Marshall and Jean Stearns' *Jazz Dance*—demonstrates this concept:

> Tucker had at the same time a disengaged and a menacing air, like a sleeping volcano, which seemed to give audiences the feeling that he was a cobra and they were mice. . . .
>
> When Snake Hips slithered on stage, the audience quieted down immediately. Nobody snickered at him, in spite of the mounting tension, no matter how nervous or embarrassed one might be. The glaring eyes burning in the pock-marked face looked directly at and through the audience, with dreamy and impartial hostility. Snake Hips seemed to be coiled, ready to strike.
>
> Tucker's act usually consisted of five parts. He came slipping on with a sliding, forward step and just a hint of hip movement. The combination was part of a routine known in Harlem as Spanking the Baby, and in a strange but logical fashion, established the theme of his dance. Using shock tactics, he then went directly into the basic Snake Hips movements, which he paced superbly, starting out innocently enough, with one knee crossing over behind the other, while the toe of one foot touched the arch of the other. At first, it looked simultaneously pigeon-toed and knock-kneed.[15]

15. *Jazz Dance* (New York: Schirmer Books, 1979; first published, 1964), p. 236.

The conflicts are paired contraries: awkward and smooth; detached and threatening; innocent and seductive. But the most significant conflict resides in the routine's deep subtext, in the ironic playing out of power postures by the otherwise disempowered black, male (dancing) body.

POLYCENTRISM/POLYRHYTHM

From the Africanist standpoint, movement may emanate from any part of the body, and two or more centers may operate simultaneously. Polycentrism diverges from the European academic aesthetic, where the ideal is to initiate movement from one locus: the noble, upper center of the aligned torso, well above the pelvis. Africanist movement is also polyrhythmic. For example, the feet may keep one rhythm while the arms, head, or torso dance to different drums. In this regard, Africanist dance aesthetics represents a democracy of body parts, rather than a monarchy dictated by the straight, centered spine. Again, we turn to "Snake Hips":

> The fact that the pelvis and the whole torso were becoming increasingly involved in the movement was unavoidably clear. As he progressed, Tucker's footwork became flatter, rooted more firmly to the floor, while his hips described wider and wider circles, until he seemed to be throwing his hips alternately out of joint to the melodic accents of the music.[16]

From a "get-down" posture that centered the movement in the legs and feet, Tucker adds the pelvis as another center, illustrating polycentrism. On top of the crossover step, described above, he interpolates a pelvic rhythm, exemplifying the simplest level of polyrhythm. Again, these are interactive principles; embracing opposing rhythms, coupled with a shifting center, demonstrates high-affect juxtaposition.

16. Ibid.

HIGH-AFFECT JUXTAPOSITION

Mood, attitude, or movement breaks that omit the transitions and connective links valued in the European academic aesthetic are the keynote of this principle. For example, a forceful, driving mood may overlap and coexist with a light and humorous tone, or imitative and abstract movements may be juxtaposed. The result may be surprise, irony, comedy, innuendo, double-entendre, and finally, exhilaration. All traditions use contrast in the arts, but Africanist high-affect juxtaposition is heightened beyond the contrast that is within the range of accepted standards in the European academic canon. On that scale, it would be considered bad taste, flashy, or loud. "Snake Hips" demonstrates this principle, in part, through his choice of costume—a sequined girdle supporting a seductive tassel:

> Then followed a pantomime to a Charleston rhythm: Tucker clapped four times and waved twice with each hand in turn, holding the elbow of the waving hand and rocking slightly with the beat. The over-all effect was suddenly childish, effeminate, and perhaps tongue-in-cheek. The next movement was known among dancers as the Belly Roll, and consisted of a series of waves rolling from pelvis to chest—a standard part of a Shake dancer's routine, which Tucker varied by coming to a stop, transfixing the audience with a baleful, hypnotic stare, and twirling his long tassel in time with the music.[17]

Tucker shifts unpredictably from childish and effeminate to challenging and "macho" movements, disregarding European standards for consistency in characterization. In addition, with

17. *Ibid.*, pp. 236–237.

no preparation or transition, he changes from light, almost cheerleader-like hand and arm gestures to weighted, sensual undulations centered in the lower torso. A third high-affect juxtaposition occurred with the "break," described above. Tucker cut off the movement in the middle of a Belly Roll, came to a break, or full stop, and shifted the mood and rhythm of his intricately structured routine.

EPHEBISM

Named after the ancient Greek word for youth, ephebism encompasses attributes such as power, vitality, flexibility, drive, and attack. Attack implies speed, sharpness, and force. Intensity is also a characteristic of ephebism, but it is a kinesthetic intensity that recognizes feeling as sensation, rather than emotion. It is "the phrasing of every note and step with consummate vitality," with response to rhythm and a sense of swing as aesthetic values.[18] The torso is flexible and articulate: "The concept of vital aliveness leads to the interpretation of the parts of the body as independent instruments of percussive force."[19] Old people dancing with youthful vitality are valued examples of ephebism in Africanist cultures. Moving with suppleness and flexibility is more important than maintaining torso alignment. Meanwhile, speed, sharpness, force, and attack are comparatively muted concepts in the European ballet tradition. (See descriptions later in this essay by Balanchine dancers, who contrast his sense of speed and timing with that found in traditional ballet.) The percussive force of independent body parts, with rhythm as a principal value, is not a part of the European ballet aesthetic.

> Tucker raised his right arm to his eyes, at first as if embarrassed (a feeling that many in the audience shared), and then, as if racked with

---

18. Thompson (1974), p. 7.
19. *Ibid.*, p. 9.

> sobs, he went into the Tremble, which shook
> him savagely and rapidly from head to foot.
> As he turned his back to the audience to dis-
> play the overall trembling more effectively,
> Tucker looked like a murderously naughty boy.[20]

Tucker's "tremble" is an excellent example of ephebism. This movement articulates the separated segments of the torso, one against the other, in a broken yet continuous movement sequence. It can be accomplished only with a totally flexible torso, which will allow the tremorlike reverberations to ripple nonstop through the body. The movement is also percussive, forceful, and intense in its attack. It racks his body. An additional fillip of ephebism is demonstrated in Tucker's "naughty boy" self-presentation.

THE AESTHETIC OF THE COOL

As Thompson so eloquently explains, the "aesthetic of the cool" is all-embracing. It is an attitude (in the sense that African Americans use that word, "attitude") that combines composure with vitality. Its prime components are visibility—dancing the movements clearly, presenting the self clearly, and aesthetic clarity; luminosity, or brilliance; and facial composure, or the "mask of the cool." The "cool" embraces all the other principles. Taken together, the sum total of all the principles can be characterized as "soul force." It is seen in the asymmetrical walk of African-American males, which shows an attitude of carelessness cultivated with calculated aesthetic clarity. It is in the unemotional, detached, masklike face of the drummer or dancer whose body and energy may be working fast, hard, and hot, but whose face remains cool. The aloofness, sangfroid, and detachment of some styles of European academic dance are completely different from this aesthetic of

---

20.   Stearns (1979/1964), p. 237.

the cool. The European attitude suggests centeredness, control, linearity, directness; the Africanist mode suggests asymmetricality (that plays with falling off center), looseness (implying flexibility and vitality), and indirectness of approach. "Hot," its opposite, is a necessary component of the Africanist "cool." It is in the embracing of these opposites, and in their high-affect juxtaposition, that the aesthetic of the cool exists.

Throughout Tucker's routine, for example, he strikes a balance between the sexual heat implied in his pelvic movements and the cool attitude of his face. Luminosity and brilliance come through in his direct relationship to the audience and the choreography, and visibility is demonstrated in the fact that he dances not as a character but as himself. These traits are valued in the Africanist aesthetic.

Some people imagine that ballet is about as far away from anything Africanist as black supposedly is from white, but things just are not as defined or clear-cut as that: not even black and white. In spite of our denials, opposites become bound together more often than we admit. Cultures borrow from each other and fusions abound.

The Africanist presence is a defining ingredient that separates American ballet from its European counterpart. Ironically, it was George Balanchine, a Russian immigrant of Georgian ethnicity, who was the principal Americanizer of ballet. Why and how is a story worth telling, even in brief. Balanchine cut his teeth as a choreographer in Europe during the Jazz Age of the 1920s. His early *Apollo* for the Diaghilev Ballets Russes exuded jazz references. After Diaghilev's death, Balanchine worked in major European cities as a ballet master and choreographed revues for the popular stage to earn a living. He also created musical routines for the first feature-length English talking film, *Dark Red Roses*, made in 1929.[21]

21. *Choreography by George Balanchine: A Catalogue of Works* (New York: Viking, 1984), p.25.

The jazz aesthetic was familiar to him before he came to the United States. Once here, he served a long apprenticeship on Broadway which helped him to assimilate popular, social, and vernacular dance influences in the service of a newly defined ballet medium. Beginning in 1936, he choreographed or co-choreographed a number of musicals, including *The Ziegfeld Follies*, *On Your Toes*, *Babes in Arms*, *I Married an Angel*, *The Boys from Syracuse*, and, with Katherine Dunham, *Cabin in the Sky*. He worked with the Nicholas Brothers, two extraordinary tap-dancing kids, in *Follies* and *Babes*, and with Josephine Baker in *Follies*. Thus, he had direct contact with African-American dancers and choreographers and with genres that were highly influenced by Africanisms.

It is already clear that Balanchine was a ballet choreographer who worked in the ballet medium and subscribed to a ballet aesthetic. What I hope to make equally clear is that, throughout his career, he introduced to the ballet canon Africanist aesthetic principles as well as Africanist-based steps from the so-called jazz dance repertory. He introduced these innovations into the ballet context while maintaining his grounding in the ballet aesthetic. The result was still ballet, but with a new accent. My guiding premises follow:

> ☐ Ballet, like all dance, is subject to the influences and presences that are valued in its cultural context. Therefore, it can rightfully be called a form of ethnic dance.
>
> ☐ Influences from past and present cultures are woven into, intermeshed with, and redistributed in any given cultural mode at any given moment in time. (To paraphrase this idea in structuralist terms, every text is an intertext.)
>
> ☐ The Americanization of ballet by a Russian immigrant, George Balanchine, will show both

African-American and European-American
influences.

□ Looking from an Africanist perspective
reveals the Africanist presence in American
ballet.

There are many places in Balanchine's ballets where the
Africanist legacy comes bursting through, most notably in the
new movement vocabulary he introduced to the ballet stage.
The displacement of hips or other parts of the torso, instead of
vertical alignment; leg kicks, attacking the beat, instead of
well-placed extensions; angular arms and flexed wrists, rather
than the traditional, rounded *port de bras*—all of these touches

George Balanchine and Arthur Mitchell rehearsing
"The Four Temperaments," 1958, photo © 1993 Martha Swope

usher the viewer into the discovery of the Africanist presence in Balanchine. These elements appear in works throughout his career and are highlighted in ballets such as *Apollo* (1928), *The Four Temperaments* (1946), *Agon* (1957), *Stars and Stripes* (1958), and *Symphony in Three Movements* (1972), among others. If and when they appeared in European ballet, these elements were reserved for lesser, "ignoble" characters and represented that which was comic or rustic, vernacular or exotic. Balanchine wielded these movements in a decidedly nontraditional fashion and assigned them central significance as movements for principals and soloists.

In the first movement of *Symphony*, the corps dancers lunge from side to side, with the straight leg turned in and one arm angularly jutting downward in a style unknown in traditional ballet. Later, a male sextet makes a prancing entrance that only can be described as an updated version of the cakewalk, with the upper torso leaning deeply backward. The second movement opens with torso isolations as a central element in the first duet, the same isolations used more baroquely in *Bugaku* (1963), which, even though it is based on a Japanese wedding ritual, reveals marked Africanist tendencies. This movement vocabulary allows Balanchine to expand the ballet idiom by introducing the articulated torso to its vertical standard.

The second and third duets of *The Four Temperaments*—the allegro tempo second duet and the adagio third—share some of the same Africanist-inflected movements. In both, ballroom dance references are as evident as the traditional pas de deux conventions into which they have been inserted. In both duets the male twirl-turns the female on one spot, as social dancers do, except that she is "sitting" in the air in *plié* while on point. The male then pumps his partner's hips forward and back as he grips her waist. He could pull her off the floor with this movement, and they would resemble Lindyhoppers. In the second duet this movement is capped off with jazzy little side lunges, straight, outstretched arms, and flexed wrists, as the two dancers face each other. And they exit with "Egyptian" arms (raised to shoulder height and bent perpendicularly from the elbow). In the third duet the male leads his partner into deep, parallel-legged squats (it would be misleading to call them *pliés*) which she performs while still on point. Then, standing, he offers his back to her. Facing his back, she wraps her arms around his neck, drapes the full length of her body against his, and leans on him. He moves forward for several steps, dragging her along. This looks like a cleaned up, slowed down variation on a typical Lindy exit. (And only in the Lindy have I seen as much female crotch as in these two duets.)

In the first variation of the "Melancholic" section a female quartet enters. Their arms are in second position, not in a traditional *port de bras*, but straight, with flexed wrists. They perform high kicks which are resolved by pushing the pelvis forward on a 1–2, kick-thrust beat, and their legs are parallel as they *bourrée* around the male. The choreography for the male is heavy, low, intense, and marked by deep lunges and acrobatic backbends. He metaphorically follows the music and "gets down"—as if this were a melancholy blues. His ephebism is balanced by the quartet's cool. He exits in a deep, acrobatic, nonacademic backbend, his outstretched arms leading him offstage, his center in his head and arms, not his spine.

There are many instances in the "Sanguinic" variation, especially in the choreography for the female soloist, where the movement is danced from the hips, which are thrust forward. This and the exit in "Melancholic," described above, are examples of the simplest version of polycentrism. Several centers are not occurring simultaneously, but the center has shifted from the vertically aligned spine to other parts of the body. The "Phlegmatic" solo opens and closes as a study in torso isolations and asymmetry. Paul Hindemith's score intimates the chords and intervals associated with blues and jazz.

Why did Balanchine incorporate these Africanist principles in his ballets? Katherine Dunham gives us a clue. "Balanchine liked the rhythm and percussion of our dances," she said, referring to her own African-American ensemble. "I think most Georgians have a good sense of rhythm from what I've seen."[22] Balanchine was the perfect catalyst for defining and shaping American ballet. The Georgian rhythmic sense that he culturally inherited was the open door that allowed him to embrace the Africanist rhythmic landscape of his new homeland. With his talent and initiative he was able to merge those two principles, just as he fused ballet's cool aloofness with the Africanist aesthetic of the cool.

The 1928 *Apollo* confirmed that Balanchine was an experimentalist and innovator in the same rank as those in literature, music, and painting who similarly reached out to African, Asian, or Oceanic vocabularies to expand their options. This ballet marked the first of Balanchine's collaborations with Igor Stravinsky who was influenced, in part, by Africanist principles in his radically rhythmic, chromatic scores. Balanchine described this work as a turning point in his career. As the three muses enter together, they perform the same high kicks with pelvis thrusting forward that reappear in *The Four Temperaments* nearly twenty years later. There is a delightful moment when they move by waddling on their heels, their legs straight. On another stage, and in another mood, that would be a tap-dance transition step. And the asymmetrical poses the dancers assume diverge from traditional ballet but are akin to Africanist dance, particularly the moving poses struck in African-American stage and social dance styles of the 1920s.

Apollo's first solo is a twisting, lunging affair. He simultaneously jumps, bends his knees so that his heels touch his

---

22.   Interview with Dunham in Francis Mason, *I Remember Balanchine* (New York: Doubleday, 1991), p. 193.

hips, and twists his hips so that they angle against his torso. His landings dig into the floor as one leg releases and kicks downward on the beat. Indeed, this solo explores the downbeat—the earth, not the air—and the soloist, like a jazz musician, hits the beat on the "one" count, not taking the preparatory "and" count that is traditional in ballet. This passage suggests a fusion between Africanisms and vernacular dance influences from Balanchine's Russian past. Another example of Balanchine's nonballetic use of phrasing and timing is recounted by Maria Tallchief, to whom he was married in the late 1940s:

> In a demonstration with Walter Terry and Balanchine, I did an eight-count *développé*, straight up and out with the *port de bras* in the manner in which we most often see it done. Then George turned to me and demanded, "Now out in *one* count and hold the rest." That is an example of the simplicity of his style. [Emphasis Tallchief's.][23]

The nontraditional timing Balanchine introduced into the ballet canon, like his introduction of the articulated torso, stretched the parameters of ballet and revitalized and Americanized the technique.

In his second solo, Apollo does several moves in which he pulls his weight off center as he lunges and stops short in an asymmetrical *plié* on the forced arch. His turns and lunges are grounded and abrupt. He stops them suddenly, as if on a dime. Unlike traditional ballet practice, the turns are not resolved: they simply stop. Both solos manifest ephebism in their speed, attack, and force. Apollo's solos and the "Melancholic" solo from *The Four Temperaments* are dances about weight and groundedness, not defying gravity but meeting it and

---

23. Mason (1991), p. 239.

embracing it. The jumps are performed not to highlight the going up, but to punctuate and emphasize the coming down. Ballet's traditional airborne quality is not present here. Instead, we find the connection to the earth characteristic of Africanist dance and American modern dance. In fact, the Africanisms evident here probably came to Balanchine through modern dance as well as social and show dance. This solo is followed by an amusing vaudeville chorus that seems to come out of nowhere. The muses join him and, with no preparation and on an abrupt change in the mood of the score, they all *plié* in an asymmetrical position, settle back into one hip with buttocks jutting out, and bounce in unison to the rhythm. They are setting time for a change in rhythm, and this is their "break." It is a radical juxtaposition, set against the previous mood and movements. It is also a quote from popular dance styles. The work ends as the three muses lean their bodies against Apollo's back, their legs in gradated arabesques, while he poses in a lunge, legs parallel, arms raised, hands flexed.

The Africanist presence in Balanchine's works is a story of particular and specific motifs, of which there are many more examples than the ones given here, from ballets that span the course of his career. In other words, these were not dispensable, decorative touches that marked one or two ballets; rather, they were essential ingredients in his canon. However, the story only begins here. More significant is the underlying speed, vitality, energy, coolness, and athletic intensity that are fundamental to his Americanization of ballet. The tale continues with the radical dynamics, off-center weight shifts, and unexpected mood and attitude changes in Balanchine's work that create a high-affect juxtaposition of elements uncommon in traditional ballet but basic to Africanist dance. Less innovative artists might have held onto the old, but Balanchine could not settle for that. He was enticed by what he saw as American qualities of speed and coolness. Of course, those qualities are predicated as much on the African presence in the Americas as the European. It simply will not suffice to say that jazz dance influenced his work. That term, jazz, has become another way to misname and silence the Africanist legacy; systematic exclusion of African Americans from American ballet has done the same. Buried under layers of deceit, that legacy in ballet has been overlooked. Some of the hidden story is intimated in Balanchine's original intentions for his new American ballet school, as recounted by Lincoln Kirstein:

> For the first [class] he would take 4 white girls
> and 4 white boys, about sixteen yrs. old and 8
> of the same, *negros* [sic]. . . . He thinks the negro
> part of it would be amazingly supple, the com-
> bination of suppleness and sense of time su-
> perb. Imagine them, masked, for example. They
> have so much abandon—and disciplined they
> would be *nonpareil*. [Emphasis Kirstein's.][24]

Thus, even before his arrival in the United States, Balanchine was calculating how he could draw upon the energy and phrasing of African Americans. Of course, the primitive trope is at work here, with the concomitant allure of the exotic. Even so, if his dream had been realized, what a different history would have been wrought for American ballet and its relationship to peoples of African lineage. One can only imagine that, innocent and ignorant of American racism, Balanchine understood, once here, that his dream school was unfeasible.

The texts that discuss Balanchine's Broadway musicals praise the ways in which he "improved" on show dancing; none of them acknowledge what he gained from that experience and took with him back to the ballet stage. But Balanchine himself may well have been aware of the two-way exchange. He said in

---

24. Letter from Lincoln Kirstein to A. Everett Austin, Jr., dated 16 July 1933, reprinted in Mason (1991), pp. 116–117.

a 1934 interview with Arnold Haskell, soon after his arrival in the United States:

> There are other ways of holding the interest [of the audience], by vivid contrast, for instance. Imagine the effect that would be produced by six Negresses dancing on their pointes and six white girls doing a frenzied jazz![25]

What he suggests, of course, is an example of high-affect juxtaposition. In working on *Concerto Barocco*, described by former New York City Ballet dancer Suki Schorer as a ballet with "a very jazzy feeling," he aimed for clarity in syncopation, timing, and attack, and he characterized a particular step as "like the Charleston."[26] His original intention for this work is expressed by former company member Barbara Walczak in her comparison of two versions of the ballet. Inadvertently, she points out Balanchine's use of the Africanist aesthetic:

> The difference between the original and today's *Barocco* is a *timing* difference, an *energy* difference. It was never meant to be lyrical. One difference was that many of the steps were *very off-center*. . . . The energy behind the steps was different. They were *attacked* more than they are now. [Emphasis mine.][27]

Patricia McBride, who danced for Balanchine from 1959 until his death in 1983, says, "Dancing Balanchine is harder—the patterns, the way they change in Balanchine ballets. The ballets are so fast, and they travel much more than a lot of the more classical companies."[28] Speed, timing, and attitude changes are key elements in Balanchine and are key to the Africanist aesthetic. They are not signature components of the ballet from which he emerged. It seems ironic that when

25. Haskell, *Balletomania Then and Now* (New York: Alfred A. Knopf, 1977), p. 98.
26. Mason (1979), p. 459.
27. *Ibid.*, p. 259.
28. *Ibid.*, p. 444.

Schorer compares the Russian ballet companies with Balanchinian ballet she states that the Russians do not understand "phrasing, counting, the timing within a step. *They've never seen anything. They only know what they know.*" [Emphasis mine.][29] What they don't know, and what Balanchine was exposed to, is the phrasing, counting, and timing that comes from the Africanist influence in American culture, so native to us that we take it for granted. By embracing these elements that he encountered in the United States, Balanchine expanded the definition of ballet. There is no doubt that his redefinition included both Africanist and European elements, fused into a spicy, pungent brew.

Balanchine's legacy, like the Africanist legacy, is a living one, much of which cannot be codified or contained by "the steps." Arthur Mitchell worked well with Balanchine, and Mitchell's cultural background and training helped. His description of *Metastaseis & Pithoprakta* shows Africanisms in Balanchine's way of working through rhythm rather than steps and in requiring the dancing body to be laid back, cool, and free to receive his messages:

> Suzanne Farrell and I danced a pas de deux that was one of those eerie things that didn't use steps per se. He'd say, "I want something like this," and he would start moving. You would just have to be free enough to let your body go and do it. I think one of the things that helped me so much with him was that, *being a tap dancer, I was used to rhythm and speed.* [Emphasis mine.] Many times when he was choreographing he would work rhythmically and then put the step in. If you were looking for a step, it wouldn't be there. But if you got

29. *Ibid.*, p. 462.

dah, da-*dah-dah-dah*, it would come out. [Emphasis Mitchell's.] The rhythm was always the most important. The choreography was set in time and then space.[30]

According to Mitchell, Balanchine sometimes referred to Dunham in his work with students and sent dancers to study with her. He also regularly called on Mitchell to "come in and show these kids, because they don't know old-fashioned jazz."[31] A final statement from Mitchell is most telling about Balanchine and the Africanist legacy:

> There was a fallacy that blacks couldn't do classical ballet—that the bodies were incorrect. But then you talked to Balanchine, who was the greatest master of them all and changed the look of ballet in the world today. He described his ideal ballerina as having a short torso, long arms, long legs, and a small head. If that's ideal, then we [peoples of African lineage] are perfect.[32]

Mitchell's quote acclaims the black dancing body, and the body is the origin and outcome of my thesis. I call this essay "Stripping the Emperor," but what needs stripping is our way of perceiving. Once we dare see the naked truth, as the child in Anderson's tale, we shall see a body, the American dancing body. It is neither black nor white.

---

30. *Ibid.*, p. 395.
31. *Ibid.*, p. 396.
32. "Talk of the Town," *The New Yorker*, 28 December 1987, 36.

LISTEN, OUR HISTORY IS SHOUTING AT US

A CHOREOGRAPHER CONFRONTS RACISM IN DANCE

Jawole Willa Jo Zollar

Once upon a time, there was a twisted, growing thing that spread throughout this great land and all over the world. No one knew how it started or where it came from, but everyone knew it had been here a long time. People were exposed to it at birth and entrenched in it by childhood. This twisted, growing thing could maim and cripple and, on all too many occasions, even kill. There were great debates about this twisted, growing thing. In fact, some people said it didn't exist at all— and if it did, it was in other people, but certainly not in them. Some people thought it was limited to regions, like it was definitely in the South, but in the North other issues were a problem—the twisted, growing thing didn't exist there. And in the West, people said, "Well, we all live together in peace and harmony, and it's certainly not here."

Now, what was really interesting about this twisted, growing thing was that it had infiltrated all the institutions in society: the schools, the churches, the banks. It was absolutely everywhere. You couldn't go anywhere without encountering it. But what was amazing was that the dance community said it didn't exist there. And I thought, "Now, how could that be if it's been everywhere else?" The dance community said the twisted, growing thing didn't exist there because the dance community had always been multiracial. I thought, "Now that's interesting."

◄ Jawole Willa Jo Zollar in Urban Bush Women's "LifeDance III … The Empress (Womb Wars)," photo by Dona Ann McAdams

If you asked a dancer like Janet Collins—who, in one period of her life had to make herself look white in order to perform, who had to "powder up," as we would say—if she thought that dance had always been multiracial and that the twisted, growing thing didn't exist there, I wonder what her response would be.

The dance community's denial of this twisted, growing thing was so deep that dance became as articulate as the rest of the nation in the language, policies, and politics of this twisted thing—but they didn't even know it because it had somehow just slipped in there. Some people didn't even want to know it.

When some of us looked at this twisted, growing thing, we noticed there were a lot of different ways of seeing how it manifested itself. And we would meet and we would talk and we would say, "Well, it's this way, it's that way." Here are some of the ways that people said this twisted, growing thing had been manifested in the dance community.

Whenever the Ailey company or the Ailey influence was written about, it was always with a slightly negative tone—so that words like "trite" and "cliché" were always present in the language. But on the other side, phrases like *chassé, pas de bourrée, pirouette,* and *thirty-two fouettés* (never thirty-one or thirty-three) were considered not trite or cliché, but classic.

When young choreographers entrenched in the traditions of their birth started working through their traditions, they caught hell from all sides. They were told, "The work is stuck in the past and it's too traditional." Or, "It's almost avant-garde, but they still stick to that narrative thing." Or, "It's angry and anger is not justified on the stage." That last one is really interesting because I've been reading the work of Native American women, and if they come to full power on the stage, the anger of African Americans is going to look like a tea party. Or they were told, "It's too abstract or culturally specific and you have to be immersed in that culture in order to know what is being said." Now that's another really interesting one. If, as an artist, you come from what some people call a "submerged culture," and you start to take the aspects of that culture and abstract them, then what do you have?

Let me offer a little scenario here as an example. Let's pretend I'm an African-American woman. I'm dressed in a big hat. I've just come from church in Harlem. I'm about sixty. I've got my high-heeled shoes on, and my suit, and my pocketbook, and I'm on my way home from church. And then you hear me doing this: [Zollar steps out and shouts "5! 632! 925! 1! 60! 295! 321!"]

Now, what was I talking about? That's right, playing the numbers. Who said that? [The speaker is African-American; the audience laughs.] Playing the numbers is an established institution in New York. It is everywhere. When I first moved there, I'd think I was going into a botanica or a little store, and I'd walk up to the door and I'd think, "It's strange that they have a buzzer." But I'd go in and say, "Is this available? Can I get this or buy that?" And they'd say, "Honey, this is a numbers joint!"

But when Laurie Carlos used that image in her piece *White Chocolate*, a lot of people asked, "What is she talking about? That's confusing. It's weird." Yet, the African-American people in New York knew exactly what that image was about. It becomes a problem when you abstract something that a lot of people don't know from direct experience. Once it's abstracted, it gets really far from the source, and the assumption is that the image is no longer cohesive.

But let's go back to how that twisted, growing thing has manifested itself in the dance community. Having audience members talk back to the performers and respond like "common cheerleaders" is something that seems to bother a lot of people. Of course, there is a cultural reason for it. But that is another manifestation of this twisted, growing thing—that some people like it when the audience talks back and other people think it's "common."

Here's another scenario. Imagine that a company comes from Ghana to perform. The curtain opens and what we see all over the stage are symbols that we understand to be swastikas. Now, in Ghana, what we call the swastika is a centuries-old symbol of the four elements, of the four directions. It's in Native American cultures, it's in Indonesian cultures, it's in Chinese cultures. But it has been made into this horrible, painful symbol in the West. So if people use that symbol on stage, what would our immediate response be?

We are used to looking at what we call the swastika from only one point of view. But it is, in fact, representative of a whole other way of thinking. It's a powerful symbol from those cultures' points of view, and a good one. But what would be written about that, and how many people would stay to find out that it had another meaning?

Under the influence of this twisted, growing thing, there was also constant denial that study was needed to understand the cultures that are right here in the United States. Everyone seems willing to acknowledge that cultures outside the United States need study and understanding. But what we often forget is that we can live side by side with someone, we can work with them, we can go out and have a drink with them, and we still may not necessarily know or understand what their culture is about.

Within the great land where this horrible, twisted, growing thing lived, there were some very well-intentioned people. Some called these people "liberals." They were appalled by this twisted, growing thing and wanted to confront it. Some did extensive work in order to confront it, deal with it, and eradicate it. Others felt that it was a problem, but said they had only a limited ability to deal with the problems. When many of these well-intentioned people took the problems on, they found that the work that needed to be done was massive, it was overwhelming, it was complicated, and it was draining.

So, out of that, and out of the conflicts with the people who were the victims of this twisted, growing thing, a whole new language was developed. Words and phrases entered our vocabulary like "culturally specific," "multicultural" (often confused with "multiracial"), "world dance," "black dance," "non-Eurocentric," "cultural equity," "cultural diversity," and "changing demographics." But in most discussions, these words were used to cover up more than they revealed. No one was willing to risk the "R" word. When the "R" word was brought up in discussions, people got crazy. So I'm carefully avoiding the use of the "R" word.

Now, in the midst of living with this twisted, growing thing, one of the positive things that started happening was that groups began to meet. Many individuals—black, white, and all colors—made a deep commitment to deal with it, me being one of them. What I discovered was this: not only was I a victim of this twisted, growing thing, but, to my surprise, I shared many of its attitudes. I didn't, however, necessarily have the power to enforce those attitudes. But if the power were to have shifted, I knew that my attitudes would reflect the twisted, growing thing.

Finding this out, I thought, "Oh, my God." So in many ways, this is the confession of a recovering—and now I'm going to use the "R" word—racist. This is a crisis in our field, and, in fact, what I am doing right now is an intervention. In dealing with this crisis of racism, I've come up with a nine-step recovery program.

My name is Jawole Willa Jo Zollar and I am a racist. I am powerless to change this pattern of thought and behavior unless I am willing to admit it exists in the first place. Can I get anyone else brave enough to join me?

[Twenty-one members of the audience respond.]

It is a powerful thing to leave denial behind and to be willing to confront those things that are very painful and deep

Zollar in "Bitter Tongue," photo by Cylla Von Tiedemann

and then to start to move forward. Here are the rest of my nine steps for recovery from racism in the dance community.

☐ I will confront the issue of linguistic racism and be willing to examine my writing from that point of view. Let's take a sports analogy, and look at studies that have compared how sports writers consider white athletes to be hardworking and intelligent, while black athletes are described as natural, gifted, and intuitive. If we were to examine the uses of language in dance writing from that point of view, what would we find?

☐ I will not, from this day forward, associate vodoun, African religions, and other indigenous spiritual forms that are earth-centered or animistic, with devil worship or demonic possession. This is a big one for us in this society, and it's very painful as a performer to read statements about your work that you know are not true.

☐ As a world citizen, I will recognize that I embrace many aesthetics, and, though I may more intensely identify with one, I will not hold that aesthetic in the superior position.

☐ I will no longer use the words "black dance" unless I am also willing to write about and talk about "white dance" and "Jewish dance." There are people like myself who don't have a problem with being identified as African-American choreographers, but it would be interesting to see white-American choreographers talked about—or Caucasian-American, or whatever that word's going to be. Soon that will be an identity crisis for somebody else to deal with.

☐ I will not confuse the ways in which American culture has been influenced by nonwhite cultures with an assumption that those cultures have had equal access to the stage.

☐ I will consider what the word "avant-garde" means in the context of traditional culture, and what it means when artists within traditional cultures experiment, whether successfully or unsuccessfully, in their own forms. One of the things we so-called "avant-garde" choreographers often talk about is that we want to be able to hang out and putz around and fail and probe without being told, "Well, the better thing to do would be to stick to the tradition." We have to understand, when artists from traditional cultures experiment, that the result may be shocking within their tradition. It may not look shocking to us. It may look like, "Well, they didn't quite make it." But, within their tradition, it may be seen as shocking and bold if you change the traditional rhythm that goes with a traditional dance. Yet the audience may not recognize that it was even done.

☐ *I will be willing to examine language patterns and ideas that generalize a group while, at the same time, figuring out what truth there may be in the generalities that are made about a particular culture.* When people say that African Americans have rhythm, why is that? Is it a rhythm gene? Is it something in the air we breathe in black communities that's different? Is our water different? Why is it that our culture uses rhythm in a very profound way? Why is it when we were performing at Dance Theatre Workshop, people said, "My God, you are all dressed so colorfully." We looked around and thought, "Well, not in my neighborhood." But then I noticed that everybody else was dressed in black; so I guess we *were* colorful.

☐ *Lastly, in whatever format I write, whether it's a monthly column, a weekly column, or a daily column, I will be willing to determine, scrupulously and honestly, how much space is devoted to artists of color versus white artists, and to alternative aesthetics versus mainstream venues and performance styles.*

I was lucky recently to be on a panel with Washington, D.C., choreographer Liz Lerman, who is part of a group called Black Artists/White Artists. They have boldly confronted issues of racism. Liz told me that, when the group first met, the black artists asked the white artists, "What is white art?" The white artists went away and they debated the issue, and they came back with this answer: White art means the privilege of never having to answer the question.

Author's note: In the time that has passed since my speech to the Dance Critics Association in August 1990, my thinking has changed on the subject of racism. Racism is an increasingly tough subject to talk about. Even to define it can lead to controversy and hysteria. The People's Institute for Survival and Beyond in New Orleans defines racism as prejudice plus power, not individual power, but institutional power. As individuals we can manifest the power of "acting out" our prejudices toward one another, but institutional power is on another level. It is the power wielded by banks and lending institutions, corporations, television and radio stations, and financial conglomerates. These institutions have the power to shape the unconscious thinking of America through the control of media (advertising; which film gets made, which doesn't; which messages are delivered, and which are not), schools, publishers, and so on and so on.

Who owns this country's major broadcasting networks? It is not African-American people. At this time, we do not hold this power. We do not control the way an advertiser depicts our relationship to white America. We do not control the money that flows through banks, nor do we control which highways get built and where (ever notice that they are always built right through African-American communities?). We do not hold the power to institutionalize racism. We do not hold the power to keep the white student from getting the scholarships or loans to colleges and universities. What we can control is the degree to which we internalize racism and oppression directed at us and the degree to which we act out on these internalized thoughts. According to the People's Institute's definition of racism—the ability to manifest it institutionally in every segment of society—African-American people do not hold the power to be racist, not yet.

We do, however, control our ability to confront these institutions on their racist practices and demand accountability. We control where our money, as consumers, is spent.

August 1994

Joan Acocella

Two recent events cast the politics of the dance community in a grim light. Both were the opening or keynote presentations of major dance-world gatherings.

At the 1990 Dance Critics Association conference, which was held in Los Angeles at the end of the summer and which had multiculturalism as its theme, the keynote address was given by the choreographer Jawole Willa Jo Zollar. In it, she spoke passionately of racism, and as the climax of her speech she made a confession, and a call for confessions. "My name is Jawole Willa Jo Zollar," she declared, "and I am a racist. I am powerless to change this pattern of thought and behavior unless I am willing to admit it exists in the first place. Can I get anyone else, anyone brave enough to join me?" After a moment of tense silence, people began calling out from the audience, "My name is so-and-so and I am a racist," "My name is such-and-such and I am a racist."

The model, I believe, was Alcoholics Anonymous. (Zollar went on to offer a nine-step recovery program.) But, of course, this was not a group of people who had come together to seek treatment for an illness. It was a group of people who had come together to talk about dance criticism. Now they were confronted with the question of whether they were "brave enough" to confess that they were racists.

This is a slightly revised version of an essay that first appeared in *Dance Ink* (July/August 1991). Reprinted with permission.

◀ *New Zealand's Waiwhetu Maori Cultural Group, photo by Janise Witt*

As it happened, not that many people did confess. According to the notes I took, there were maybe twelve,[1] but among them were important people, people with jobs at major universities, major newspapers, major funding organizations. They called out their names and declared themselves racists.

This, I believe, was an attack on language and therefore on truth. The word "racist" means something. It means someone who believes that other racial groups, by virtue of their race, are inherently inferior, with the implication that those groups should be denied privileges granted to other, "superior" groups. As we know, certain people *are* racists, and the term should be reserved for them, so that we know what we are dealing with. I don't know whether Zollar is a racist—I doubt it—but I do know that many of the people who joined her in her confession are not racists. They know it, too. If you told them they were racists, they would be very insulted. If you told their employers that they were racists, they would call their lawyers, and well they might, for racism is a serious charge.

And that is what was being denied here. Like other social attitudes, racism has a thousand gradations, a thousand traces in our lives. But what is the "racism" to which these people were confessing? The time they said "nigger" and "honkie" when they were five? The time they attended a de facto segregated elementary school? The time they were amused or annoyed at some ethnically specific behavior because it was different from what their ethnically specific experience taught them was proper? Shall we call Richard Pryor racist because he makes fun of the way white people talk? If so, what will we call George Wallace? We will have no meaningful term left.

And that is the effect of these group confessions: to undo all the hard work of distinction making—work that takes brains and morals—and to plunge us all into an ecstacy of self-blame,

---

1. David Gere listened to an audiotape of this session and counted twenty-one.

which, because it is collective, is less painful. In fact, as many have reported, it doesn't feel half bad. That is why it has been used not just by Alcoholics Anonymous but also by many totalitarian regimes—the Chinese Communists were famous for their confession sessions—and also by many of the evangelical sects that form the backbone of the "religious right." In the moment of confession, one's sinfulness seems purged. In any case, the way to salvation seems clear, for it is there in the hands of the authority who is extracting the confession. How utterly remote all this is from the complex and insidious problem of racism should be obvious.

A subtext of such public confessions is that we are all guilty: the difference between those who stand up and those who don't is not a difference of guilt but a difference of courage. As Zollar said, "Can I get anyone brave enough to join me?" This suggestion does not seem to have worked that well at the DCA conference. It was more insisted upon, and more effective, at a second big dance-world convocation two weeks after the DCA conference: the 1990 Bessie Awards ceremony, which took place in New York City on September 12.

As most people will remember, the Bessie Awards occurred at the peak of the censorship controversy that was kicked off by the cancellation of the Robert Mapplethorpe show at the Corcoran Gallery in the summer of 1989 and then the denial of the NEA grants to Karen Finley, Holly Hughes, Tim Miller, and John Fleck in the summer of 1990. Karen Finley was to have been one of the two cohosts of the Bessies, and Holly Hughes was to give the performance that would open the show. Then, two weeks before the ceremony, Finley withdrew, on the grounds that the Bessies received funding from Philip Morris, which had been a major contributor to the election campaigns of Jesse Helms and had just given a large grant toward the construction of a museum in honor of Helms. (That, a few weeks before the Bessies, Finley had performed in the Philip

Morris–supported Serious Fun festival at Lincoln Center and, one week after the Bessies, was to open a season at the Philip Morris–supported Joyce was an inconsistency that was never explained, as far as I know.) A week after Finley withdrew, her cohost, the actress Danitra Vance, also withdrew. They were replaced, and the Bessies went on, but in an atmosphere of terrible strife.

As it turned out once the ceremony started, Holly Hughes had also withdrawn, or sort of. The press release had said she would perform, and there she was in the printed program, as the first event: "*When Push Comes to Shove*, Holly Hughes." But what happened instead—I was later told that it was scripted by Hughes—was the following. A man and a woman came onstage in street clothes and addressed the audience. "I'd like everyone in the audience who is gay or lesbian, a fag or a dyke or a queer, to please stand," the woman said. According to my notes, about half the audience stood up. Then she said, "Now I'd like everyone who has ever slept with anyone of the same sex to please stand," and some more people stood. Then she asked "everyone whose work contains gay or lesbian content" to join those standing, and some more people stood up. Then those of us who had failed to stand were told to think about Rosa Parks, the Stonewall riot, and other historical occasions where people either stood or did not stand by others who were being made to suffer unjustly. We were told how King Christian of Denmark had a yellow star sewn on his jacket when the Nazis declared that the Danish Jews had to wear yellow stars. (As was recently pointed out in a letter to the *New York Review of Books* by a representative of the Danish royal family, King Christian never did this.) "If we are a community," said the man onstage, "why are some of us sitting?"

Actually, by this time a lot of the people who had stood up were now sitting again. Some of them probably just got tired, but others may have been uncomfortable with what was going on here, which was a public shaming. Either you declared yourself as belonging to one of the three announced categories—(1) gay, (2) veteran of at least one homosexual experience, (3) artist or critic whose work dealt with homosexuality, presumably as a major subject—or you had forsaken, in their struggle, those who fell into these categories. It didn't matter what else you were. What about the writers who addressed homosexuality if it was an important question in the art but who didn't regard it as one of their big subjects? What about the people who considered their sexual history a private matter? Were there any nuns in the audience? No matter. In the words of Eldridge Cleaver, you were either part of the solution or part of the problem.

It was a hard moment. I was sitting with a close friend, and he stood up when the first category was announced. As the speakers went through the remaining categories and then the historical lessons—Rosa Parks, the Jews—I looked at him, standing, and he looked at me, sitting, the two of us now defined as different, and on different sides. It was ridiculous. It was also cruelly separatist and flatly in violation of the truth.

The implied claim here is that people who belong to a group that has suffered have the right to define reality for others, if only on these expiatory occasions. They don't. Furthermore, I wonder how much of the audience is actually taking the speakers' words seriously, as opposed to just giving them what they seem to want. If the DCA keynote address had been given by a white person, there would probably have been far fewer confessions of racism. Likewise, at the Bessie ceremony, I *know*, because they told me afterward, that a number of people stood up on the last call just because they saw where things were going and they weren't about to get caught sitting down at the end. If the speakers hadn't announced themselves as gay, this "Aw, hell" quotient would probably have been a lot lower.

"Just look at my painting and Become a Human Being," wrote Karen Finley in a recent piece in *Artforum*. "Just read my book and Change." As it happens, many people are already human beings, without exposure to Finley's work. When, at the Bessies, the dividing of the sheep from the goats was over, the two people who replaced Finley and Vance as cohosts— performance artist Jerri Allyn and actress–performance artist Laurie Carlos—came onstage. Carlos took the mike and said, "You know, some of us ain't none of those things they said before. Some of us are just sisters. I'd hate to think that I was part of a sect."

Here Carlos put her finger on the basic problem, sectarianism, an old error for which multiculturalism and the dividing of gay and nongay are only the most recent arenas of potential support. In both cases the idea is that by virtue of falling into some subgroup, defined by race or sexual preference or whatever, we are automatically rendered incapable of understanding people in other groups. This, I think, was what underlay those confessions of racism at the DCA conference. What the people were declaring themselves guilty of was not racism in its dictionary sense—as I said, the ones I know are by no means guilty of it—but what they were assuming to be a built-in incomprehension and hostility among races. In other words, they were acceding to the multiculturalist argument that ethnic origin truly and inevitably separates people. The same goes for the opening of the Bessie Awards. The assumption was that people who have had no homosexual experience or (last chance, now) have not made homosexuality a major concern of their work are significantly alienated from those who have, to the point where they cannot share their values, see their point, understand their art.

In the face of such an argument, arts criticism simply comes to a halt. If I say that the late work of Alvin Ailey was clichéd— Zollar in her keynote address complained of such criticisms of

Ailey—that is just my ethnic bias operating. If Kim Sagami, of the Joffrey Ballet, takes on the role of the Young Girl in Kurt Jooss' *Green Table*, then we have to send a Japanese-American critic to the theater to find out whether or not she's good. But then we would also have to send—what? an Aryan, right?—to understand Jooss' choreography. We would also have to send a Jew, to judge Fritz Cohen's score. But wait—what's Kim Sagami doing in a Caucasian ballet anyway? How can she understand it if she's of Asian origin? Of course, it was exactly such racial arguments, in his case imposed by the Nazis, that caused Jooss to make *The Green Table* in the first place and then to exile himself from Germany, his native land, for sixteen years.

Racial arguments do not hold up. Alvin Ailey's late work *was* clichéd, and you don't have to have a Japanese grandmother to see that Kim Sagami did a good job in *The Green Table*. I have been writing about the work of gay, black, and Asian-American artists, with what I take to be justice, for ten years. (Others have been doing it for a lot longer.) In the process, I have never had to enter into long discussions of homosexuality or race, and the suggestion that such discussion is called for simply because the artist in question is gay, black, or Asian-American is a form of prejudice. Artists are of course affected by being black or white, gay or straight—male or female, too—but to categorize and label their work accordingly is to imply that what makes us different from one another outweighs what makes us alike, and able to understand. Zollar in her speech objected to discussions of "black dance" in the absence of any discussion of "white dance." So should we all object, to both terms. For if at this moment sectarian arguments do not hold up, eventually they could. That is, the hostility they generate could eventually divide people to the point where in truth they no longer understand one another, or want to.

WHAT IS CLASSICISM?

Alastair Macaulay

with reviews by Sal Murgiyanto, Christine Temin, Deborah Jowitt, Lewis Segal, Gus Solomons jr, Judith Green, Jack Anderson, Marcia B. Siegel, Paul Parish, Allan Ulrich, and Nicole Plett and Barbara Figge Fox

I am an experienced critic and I read a lot of reviews, but I believe it is not my business to tell other critics how to write a review. I do, however, have some priorities. I don't think that criticism is a form of social science or anthropology, though I think it frequently overlaps with those things and should do so. I don't think that criticism is an endeavor to communicate the intention of an artist or the systems of a different culture—though again it will often overlap with those things and can be valuable for doing so. I certainly don't think I have to go to Java to prepare for a performance of Javanese *Bedhaya*. I'm a working critic with several deadlines every week. I cannot go to every nation to do my swatting up for all the dances I am going to see—not if I'm writing four or five reviews a week, or one a week, or even two a month. If and when I go to various countries, I do what work I can. I learn from that. I use it. Most of the time, I'm just a working critic going from one deadline to the next.

This presentation was given the day after a performance of the Court Art of Java from the Kraton of Yogyakarta. The performance, presented by the Festival of Indonesia and the 1990 Los Angeles Festival, took place at the Los Angeles Arboretum on 31 August 1990.

◀ *Bedhaya Arjuna Wiwaha at the Yogyakarta palace, Java, photo © Linda Vartoogian*

I'm saying all of this because many people seem to suppose that the critic starts from knowledge, that what got him the job in the first place is that he has more information than the average person. Let me suggest that, in fact, a good starting point for a critic is ignorance—or, rather, the recognition that he or she is ignorant. The first tool for a critic is not knowledge or research but sensibility. I like to have information. But I also know, as any researcher does, that I'm never going to have enough of it. And so I just have to start writing without all of the facts at my fingertips.

In seeing Javanese *Bedhaya* for the first time, for instance, I chose not to use a headset for translation. My reason was not that I disdained the information. I'd love to see that performance again with a headset. But I wanted to experience the music for the first time without any interference, any commentary. Lord knows that opera supertitles are controversial enough. Headsets I think are something else again.

So here is my overnight review.

The gamelan orchestra, its instruments so beautifully carved and shaped, stretches against the back of the stage for Javanese dance theater. This is music as decor. So much is already apparent from watching and listening to the players. They sit, visible only above the waist, like the forty thieves half out of their jars. There is no conductor, and the players face in different directions—most to the front, but some sideways, and one or two with their backs to us. There is no great stress or excitation. They play calmly, impassively, as if things have always been so. Composure, sitting, facing in four different directions, impersonal participation: these qualities all are evident in the dancing that followed.

To me, the evening's greatest pleasure of all was the relatively familiar gamelan sound world. The bells, chimes, and gongs form the softest percussion imaginable. Those tintinnabulations have a rippling quality. Often, in fact, they sound like bells left hanging in the wind: an Aeolian music, like the harp that is played by the breeze. This is music, to my ear, like a strange forest without danger. It has space, light, and no pressure of getting on from A to B, let alone to Z. (The gamelan has entered into our Western musical bloodstream. Last night I was reminded of Ravel's *Mother Goose Suite*, of Benjamin Britten's score for *The Prince of the Pagodas*, and of his dance music for the character Tadzio in the opera *Death in Venice*.) The more marked chimes deal out steady, even, impersonal melodies; and when in tensely dramatic moments in the evening's second work, the *Golek Menak*, there is an occasionally loud tapping anvil noise, it seems to try to interrupt—or, rather, it sounds like a bird's alarm call.

Surely nothing stays in the memory from the whole evening more indelibly than the entrance and exit of the nine women of the *Bedhaya*—the slow, processional drag-march, planting the bare foot firmly on the floor with flexed toes pointing up. When the weight is fully placed on the front foot, it's a major event, and, during their exit, it's precisely, solemnly signaled by gamelan chimes. Only a walk, yet how momentous.

Elsewhere in the work, the women travel in a quick soft pitter-patter that matches the ripples in the music, too; and gradually we realize that the many elements in the dance all find their match in the web of the music. Everything, in fact, seems preordained. The sense of ceremony is constant. What a wonderful shock to discover, late in the forty-five-minute work, that embedded amid all the composure and calm and formal geometry is a story. The group of women subdivides; and we see the many, the few, the one. Daggers are produced from sheaths, though at first they might as well be fans. Then, as lightly as when Ginger slaps Fred in the "Night and Day" duet in *The Gay Divorcee*, one woman darts her dagger into the other and sends her softly reeling across the stage, where she composes herself in what I take to be the final sitting position of defeat and death. You can read the full narrative in the program.

But the dance passes on, and the two combatants merge back into the ensemble. The daggers were really no more important than the purple-pink plumes on the women's heads, or the long scarves around their waists, which they furl and unfurl as they proceed, or the endlessly fascinating gesticulation of their fingers—held in one dance together, elsewhere parted, flexed, or bent. The *Bedhaya* is, I suppose, a slow dance. At one point, during the time it took for a plane to pass overhead, the one dancer who was then in transit scarcely covered more than two feet while the plane went right across the sky.

Yet one's feeling while one watches is of economy and concentration. Within all the impersonal restraint, there is always intentness, suspense, tension, vital essence. When the nine dancers all slowly tilt diagonally sideways, like little leaning towers; when the lines of kneeling or pacing women face variously north, south, east, or west; when the kneeling women, with their hands, keep up a choral commentary on the central action; and when necks, fingers, toes, legs all play so crucial a role, we're made aware how tightly something has been distilled.

It is not hard for an Englishman to cherish such an angelically stiff-upper-lip attitude to matters of life and death, and so rigorous a belief in formality and courtesy at all times. It is not hard for a Merce Cunningham devotee to love such an emphasis on private space encompassing each human being. It is not hard to see accidental connections between the formal geometric floor patterns and impersonal feeling of these court dances and what we know of the Renaissance and French Baroque court dances that were the cradle of ballet.

The *Bedhaya* seems at once to show many of the principles

of classicism. It places formal etiquette and elegance above communication of meaning, it demonstrates a belief in order and composure, it displays a complex overall structure of rhythm, gesture, and movement whereby sight and sound are consistently and coherently connected, and whereby each detail is made vital in terms of time and space. We see, above all, a code of manners—not apparently adapted at all to Western ways. Often, curiously, the *Bedhaya* code satisfies most when least we can decode it.

Having written that review, I would, if I were going on to compose a further essay, pursue other points. I'll set them before you now:

My first feeling is that I would describe more intensely. There is yet more in that movement for me to get across. Secondly, I would proceed to describe the *Golek Menak*, the dance-drama form that completed the evening. That would invite me to tackle a whole other range of issues. *Golek Menak* is more obviously a varied form, and it has various different forms within it. I notice particularly a more marked kind of recitative, both singing and speech, and various kinds of related mime movement. For those, and other reasons, it seems to me a less formally perfect work, and therefore I would come into further issues of evaluation and of daring to find fault with a performance about which I am, as I say, uncertain and ignorant.

I would pursue, I think, the idea of the story in the *Bedhaya*, which to me, the day after the performance, is of secondary interest. I would investigate the *Mahabharata* further and therefore try to enter into a more interpretative form of criticism, to see how it got its meaning across. This wasn't high on my priorities.

The idea of different forms of classicism seems to me an important one for a critic to investigate, in part because

Golek Menak at the Yogyakarta palace, photo © Linda Vartoogian

classicism is itself multicultural. The classicism that we recognize in ballet seems to have originated in twin principles: the idea we find in Homer that embedded in the human is something divine and that gods are active in human warfare and human love and human conduct; and the idea we find in Genesis that God created humankind in God's own image. Is that so when we look at the different classicism of Javanese culture? What I don't see is that outwardness of impulse, that openness, the sense that the body radiates into infinity. There is a more inward concentration that has different moral suggestions for all of us.

I would like to introduce a point I heard at the 1989 Dance Critics Association conference in San Francisco where we saw performances by a flamenco dancer, a Balinese dancer, an Indian dancer, and an African dancer, after which we heard them talk about each other's forms and their own forms. Later, we also heard a panel of critics and anthropologists discussing what they had seen.

On the whole, the assumption throughout was that one form was as good as another. But do we really think so? Certainly I think we have more difficulties with one form than another. I am more familiar with African dance than with Javanese, but I also sense in it a greater disparity of spirit. A clue to this was given to me by I Wayan Dibia, the Balinese dancer. He said that, while he admired all the other dances he saw at the conference, for Balinese dancing there is a set of criteria, and that one criterion was repose. There must be an element of repose in the dance.

Now I recognize this element as a quality I value in ballet; it's something I also love in Cunningham and various other of the dance forms I review. To me, in African dancing, there is something—for lack of a better word—Dionysian. It keeps on going with a permanent attack, almost abandon. At least, that's how it looks to my kind of restraint. I recognize that, I admire it, but I also recognize that its Dionysian aspect puts it at a distance from me. I can't participate in it spiritually. And maybe, if I'm pushed, I can't say I enjoy it blissfully. Actually, I'm fascinated by African dance music, I can always go on analyzing the music and so forth, but there is a degree to which I do stand back from it; and, in my experience, the dance is considerably less interesting than its accompaniment.

One needn't apply this only to alien cultures. I'm endlessly crazy about flamenco; I can't get enough of it. But if there's a folk dance form I see even more of, it's Morris dancing, and to be truthful it bores me rigid. So one is not necessarily talking about otherness here. Morris dancing, like a lot of British folk dance forms, is frankly very limited. I don't think, therefore, that the word "other" is always the issue. Sometimes we find limitations in our own backyard.

I don't think of myself as a daily paper critic, but I've been at the moment forced into it, and it's actually a very good challenge. The refreshing part of it is that, if you want to communicate with your idea of a daily paper's readers, you describe a lot. You try to emphasize just what you saw to your average, untutored reader. I think maybe in writing for a more specialized audience you can go straight on to further complex issues of interpretation and analysis and evaluation. Evaluation must be there, but I think particularly for a daily paper, I would stress the descriptive quality.

If you remember, my priority is that you operate with your sensibility. That's the first point. And that you describe with your sensibility. In my *Bedhaya* review, I left some things undescribed because, under pressure, I couldn't yet formulate how I had responded. When I was aware of how my feeling connected to what I saw, I put it down. There were, however, moments when I thought, "I know what I saw, but I don't yet quite know how I felt about it." But this can be true of any dance.

I should point out simply that the review I've given here is a review I can write only once. Next time, I'll have seen that much more Javanese dance. That will be my knowledge, I will build upon that. We all get less and less ignorant about each form. Maybe we get, therefore, a bit more arrogant as we get more knowledgeable, but we should remind ourselves as critics—also just as communicating members of human society—that ignorance is, and should be, our starting point.

The following review was written by the Indonesian critic Sal Murgiyanto in 1977.

SAL MURGIYANTO[1]

On September 6–8, the Siswo Among Bekso Dance Troupe from the Court of Yogyakarta revisited Jakarta presenting two different programs at the Arena Theater. Though their performance of *Wayang Topeng* in the opening and closing nights was rather shaky, the *Bedhaya* in the second evening was a delight.

Bedhaya is a four-hundred-year-old dance form that has been neglected since the rise of the Ramayana Prambanan *Sendratari* (a dance-drama without dialogue) in Yogyakarta in 1961.

There are similarities between *Bedhaya* and *Sendratari*. Both have narrative themes, are performed by many dancers, and are accompanied by vocal and instrumental gamelan music with no dialogue. But there are characteristics that belong to *Bedhaya* alone. For example, all nine dancers in *Bedhaya* are female. Each of these dancers has a name—*batak, endel, dada, jangga, endel weton, apit ngajeng, apit wingking, apit meneng,* and *buncit*—but these names do not represent a specific character

---

1. Excerpted and adapted from "Bedhaya Dance: Reflection on the Glory of the Past," *Kompas* (Jakarta, Indonesia) (27 September 1977). Original translation by Sal Murgiyanto.

or role as in *Sendratari*. Instead, they denote a specific placement or position in conventional *Bedhaya* floor patterns, or
Rakit. Furthermore, *Sendratari* costumes are designed to differentiate characters. In *Bedhaya* all dancers wear identical costumes.

In *Bedhaya*, a female dancer may "act out" a male role in a
love scene or a fight scene, but she never transforms herself
into the "strong male" dance mode. From beginning to end,
Bedhaya dancers remain in their female mode, which is elegant, subtle, and refined.

According to Javanese tradition, the oldest and the most
sacred of all *Bedhaya* is the *Bedhaya Ketawang*, believed to have
been created by Sultan Agung, the "Great Sultan" of Mataram,
who reigned 1613–1645, to commemorate the sacred relationship between Panembahan Senopati, founder of the Mataram
Dynasty, 1586–1601, and Kanjeng Ratu Kidul. It is said that,
through a deep meditation, Panembahan Senopati was once
able to meet the Goddess of the South Sea. During the encounter at her palace at the bottom of the ocean, the Goddess
expressed her sincere love to Senopati and asked him to stay
and reign over her kingdom. The handsome king politely re-
fused the plea, but agreed to marry her—even promised that
all his successors would do the same. Then he asked the
Goddess to visit his palace in Mataram. During her first visit,
she taught the *Bedhaya Ketawang* to a group of selected female
court dancers. She returned to her own palace but regularly
visited Mataram to meet Senopati and observe the *Bedhaya
Ketawang* rehearsals.

Today the *Bedhaya Ketawang* has become a sacred heirloom
and a grand ritual at the Court of Surakarta (a neighboring
court of Yogyakarta) and is performed once a year, during the
commemoration of the anniversary of the ruler's ascension to
the throne. Its rehearsals are conducted only on the day of
Selasa Kliwon in the Javanese calendar, which occurs every
thirty-five days.

In the ritual performance of *Bedhaya Ketawang*, the dancers must be physically and mentally clean. For example, if one of the dancers is menstruating, she must stop rehearsing and be replaced. Various offerings must be properly prepared for the rehearsals and performance to ward off bad luck.

Almost every sunan of Surakarta and sultan of Yogyakarta has ordered his dance masters to create his own *Bedhaya*. The incorporation of a narrative theme in *Bedhaya* compositions seems to have occurred later, since older *Bedhaya*s are usually named after the accompanying gamelan melody such as *Bedhaya Pangkur* and *Bedhaya Sinom*. Only later, there emerged *Bedhaya Bedah Madiun* ("Invasion of Madiun") and *Bedhaya Seyambara Sinta* ("Contest to Win Sita"), which are called, respectively, *Bedhaya Gondokusumo* and *Bedhaya Purwotejo* after the particular *gending* (gamelan composition) that accompanies each dance.

The late Prince Hadiwijaya from the Court of Surakarta once stated that *Bedhaya* originated in pre-Hindu-Javanese time. During the Hindu-Javanese period, *Bedhaya* developed as a temple dance; when Islam came to Java, *Bedhaya* moved into Javanese courts as both ritual and entertainment (or *klangenan*) for royalty.

Like other Yogyanese *Bedhaya*, the *Bedhaya Purwotejo* performed by the Siswo Among Bekso Dance Troupe consists of three parts: the entrance, the *Bedhaya* proper, and the exit. The entrance and the exit sections are traditionally called *kapang-kapang*, a formal walking step for dancers to enter or leave the performance area in the court. These two sections are always accompanied by a gamelan composition called *gending kapang-kapang*, which incorporates the playing of some Western drums (*tambur*). *Harjuno Asmoro*, one type of *gending kapang-kapang*, accompanies the entrance; *Harjuno Rangsang* accompanies the exit.

The *Bedhaya* proper consists of two sections. The first is a pure dance composition based on *Bedhaya* conventions and is

accompanied by three melodies: Bowo Sekar Sarimulat (an opening song by a female vocalist), Gending Purwotejo, and finally,
Ladrang Sidomukti. All three pieces are played in Pelog Barang key.

This first section does not tell a story but provides more
room for presenting floor patterns such as rakit lajur, rakit tiga-
tiga, and rakit urut kacang. The nine dancers provide the possibility of endless varieties of floor patterns, both symmetrical
and asymmetrical. From one rakit to the next, transitions are
flowing, without abrupt stops or "rough" movements.

Both the first and the second sections begin with the dancers sitting cross-legged (lenggah sila). When the musicians begin to play the gamelan, the nine dancers slowly rise and
perform smooth, flowing movements following the rhythm
and the mood of the accompaniment. When the gamelan
ends (suwuk), the movement also ends calmly.

Rusli, a well-known painter, member of the Academy of
Jakarta, and long-time Yogyakarta resident, commented that
today's choreographer could learn a great deal from watching
the Bedhaya Purwotejo. "Good choreography is not just an as-
sembling of different dance movements in various ways," Rusli
says. "In many new works, variety predominates—even de-
stroys unity."

Indeed, the night I saw the Siswo Among Bekso Troupe, the
Bedhaya Purwotejo, which was marked predominantly by continuous, slow, flowing movements, seemed not dull at all, the
result of the richness of the composition, the dignity of the
singing, and the ritualistic gamelan melodies.

In Bedhaya there is a narrative theme, elegant and refined
body movement, gamelan and vocal music, but Bedhaya differs
markedly from the newly created Sendratari dance drama. Bedhaya
presents beautiful movements which are, to quote the late
Prince Suryobrongto, "symbolic and abstract."

Unlike Sendratari, Bedhaya does not tell a story through gesticulation or distract its audience by presenting movement

tricks, realistic gestures, and acrobatic feats. Rather, *Bedhaya* is distinguished by slow, meditative, flowing movements that awaken one's sensitivity and inner feelings. This is the beauty of *Bedhaya*.

Today, many Javanese have traded *Bedhaya* for *Sendratari*, which is narrative, realistic, and easy to understand. But *Bedhaya Purwotejo* is a reflection of the glory of the past.

> *The dozen excerpts that follow are from articles written in 1990 by American critics. All were written in response to an abridged version of Bedhaya Arjuna Wiwaha performed by Court Art of Java, a special Festival of Indonesia company from Yogyakarta. Christine Temin's piece was filed from Java, the others from various cities on the American tour.*

CHRISTINE TEMIN[2]

The most breathtaking work in our abbreviated performance was the *Bedhaya*, performed by nine identically dressed females: Traditionally, they included relatives of the sultan. A category of dance with many variations, the *Bedhaya* is about spiritual unity, expressed through the almost painfully slow unison movement of the women, who walk onstage heel-first, unfurling their feet until their toes meet the floor. It's an extraordinarily voluptuous image. We lost all sense of time during the hypnotic dance. When it stopped, we felt as if we had been watching for perhaps twenty minutes. It turned out to have been forty-five minutes, the length Americans will see. The original was two or three hours; currently in Java the *Bedhaya* is generally an hour and a half.

We all wished we had seen a three-hour version of the beguiling *Bedhaya*, a dance without any of the sensationalism of many Western forms, a dance whose purity seems to

2. "Dance of Life," *Boston Globe Magazine* (16 September 1990).

symbolize an ideal way of life. Accustomed as they are to abstraction, Americans may well take to the *Bedhaya* as Indonesians, we're told, have not.

DEBORAH JOWITT[3]

In the Arboretum in Arcadia, a simulated marble platform has been set up on the lawn and further dappled with light (by Stan Pressner). Wooden pillars support a roof to shelter the gamelan of the Royal Court of Yogyakarta. Behind is a vista of green. In the distance, where steps lead up to another lawn and a reflecting pool, we can see the dancers in their gilt headdresses, velvet jackets, batik drapes, and red sashes as they cross to make a new entrance.

The nine women who perform the eighteenth-century *Bedhaya* mount the steps to the stage in strict formation. Their backs and legs are straight, their eyes modestly downcast; one delicately curled hand stretches the loose end of batik out to the side. Contained and unhurried, they walk, each foot circling the other, toes raised, before it gently, firmly settles on the floor. It is one of the world's great walks. They step into the complicated shimmer and twinkle of the gamelan like fine boats floating down a bubbling river—traveling without seeming to move.

But when they arrive in place and turn to face us (including the sultan in a Western dark suit), they soften. Now their knees bend, and they lean slightly forward or, almost perilously, tilt sideways; now their hands, with curling fingers or flat, arching palms trace decorous patterns on the air or flip the ends of their sashes. I'm aware of a constant, subtle rising and sinking; when they curve one leg very slightly forward and then wreathe it back around the other leg to touch just the ball of the foot on the floor, the action has the force of a quiet, satisfied sigh.

Embedded in the dreamy ceremonious patterns of this

---

3. "Melting-Pot Pacific," *Village Voice* (18 September 1990).

Bedhaya is a story—highly abstracted—taken from the epic *Mahabharata*. It tells of Arjuna (meditating in the guise of the monk Ciptoning) who, aided by the celestial nymph Supraba, obliges the gods by tricking and killing the demon king Niwatakawaca (who had the nerve to demand Supraba for his bride). Arjuna and Supraba are then married. In the *Bedhaya*, this story becomes simply a matter of shifts in the classical patterning. A woman steps and sways in the center: the meditating god. Two women circle each other: a partnership is formed. Pairs of women lean toward one another in loveseat position, each holding a small dagger: a fierce battle. One woman flicks her dagger lightly but sharply toward the throat of another: the hero aims at the villain's vulnerable palate. A dancer may represent Ciptoning one moment, Niwatakawaca the next. The events of the drama have been transcribed into elegant shorthand. And then the women slowly, magically, sail on across the platform down the steps, and onto the darkening grass.

LEWIS SEGAL[4]

"Beautifully accomplished, the Bedhaya dancers; cultivated in the art of dance, they are ready. . . ."

The opening chorus in the "Court Art of Java" program, at the Los Angeles State and County Arboretum last Friday, told you exactly what to expect. Here, in an American premiere, came the embodiment of a Central Javanese palace tradition renowned for its accomplished, cultivated artistry.

Before an opening night L.A. Festival audience that included the Sultan of Yogyakarta himself, a group of nine women in sleeveless crimson jackets over brown and white batik sarongs appeared "slowly walking . . . their clothes glittering with jewels" (in the words of the text), ". . . every movement perfectly timed."

---

4. "'Court of Java' Delivers Promised Mastery," *Los Angeles Times* (3 September 1990).

Ever since the seventeenth century, *Bedhaya* dancers have walked this way into the presence of their sultans—their left hands holding their sarongs out from their bodies, their empty right hands identically placed and, with each step, their feet swiveling outward as their toes curled up.

Even before any actual dancing began on Friday, this regal procession onto an outdoor platform stage (the musicians seated at the rear) suggested something of Yogyakarta court decorum as well as defining the concentration on unison activity—nine women moving as one—that *Bedhaya* ritualizes into a metaphysical quest.

Shifting formations and patterns of synchrony traced the path toward oneness and as the women swayed, or sank into their weight, or flicked the ends of their long, red sashes into the air, their flow of motion generated something as elusive yet tangible as a gentle undersea current.

Bedhaya Arjuna Wiwaha at the Yogyakarta palace,
photo by Rachel Cooper

Every delicate tilt of head and other small displacement continually seemed the result of a surge generated by the dancers' larger actions. Impulses traveled through empty air as easily as bodies, binding the nine together—fusing them in space.

Midway through came evocations of *Arjuna Wiwaha* (*Arjuna's Wedding*), an episode from the Hindu epic *Mahabharata* with its own statement about self-denial. Such gestural elements as daggers stabbed into the air provided signposts identifying moments in the narrative, but the dancers never really enacted the roles they briefly assumed. Instead, they functioned as ritual implements: tracing the pattern, but detached from the motion—far away from us in meditation.

GUS SOLOMONS JR[5]

Nine women move together, inching across the stage, drawing us almost magically into their aura of serenity. They glide like swans on still water, their focus demurely downcast, in a formation representing at once the human body with its nine orifices and the nine human desires. The movement is immaculately executed: a foot circles to the rear, gathering with it the trailing tail of the stiff, wrapped skirt, and stamps a gentle punctuation behind the supporting leg; the knees bend into a curtsey.

Articulate hands gesture with fingers arched back or crooked into delicate curlicues, then slip under floor-length red sashes and lightly flick them into the air to mark the end of each seamless movement phrase. The action is choreographed down to the tiniest shift of a glance, yet each dancer breathes life into her individual performance as if animated by a transcendent spirit.

One is struck by the parallels between this royal court dance and classical ballet. Both are precise, exacting, highly

5. Unpublished review (1990).

codified techniques that use symbolic gestures to narrate tales of legend and fantasy. In both, the dance and music are closely wedded; both are presentational rather than participatory; both originated in royal courts. The similarities to a familiar form allow us westerners more easily to enter the realm of this exotic form. Once there, however, we find the sensibilities of the two forms different indeed. The Javanese dance is a composite of nuances: tiny gestures, emotional subtleties, repose, and restraint.

JUDITH GREEN[6]

Nine women step lightly onto a platform stage, placing their feet precisely and elegantly on its floor.

The feet move heel first, the sole well arched. With every step, the foot stretches through the arch until the toes are finally on the floor, the movement taking only seconds to execute.

One woman steps up. Behind her, another. Behind her, three abreast. Behind them, three more. Behind them, one. In formation, they resemble a small armada, skimming serenely across the smooth surface of the stage.

When they change their pattern, their swift, silent bare feet make no more sound than a few dry leaves blown by the wind. In minimal movements, they regroup in a circle or split their ranks—three women kneeling on this side and four standing on that—to flank a pair of soloists.

They are dressed identically in red and gold skirts of polished cotton, imprinted with a stylized bird in flight; red velveteen vests trimmed with gold metallic fringe; red-and-white-patterned sashes; gold belts, arm bands, breastplates; gold tiaras with pink maribou plumes fastened above the brows; delicate gold hair ornaments, like anemone buds trembling on long, golden stems.

---

6. "Javanese Fest Features Silent Steps," *San Jose Mercury News* (13 September 1990).

This is *Bedhaya*, a classical Javanese court dance of the seventeenth century.

JACK ANDERSON[7]

Bedhaya, an all-female form dating from the seventeenth century, was represented by *Arjuna Wiwaha* (*Arjuna's Wedding*). . . . The *Bedhaya* treatment of this traditional story was virtually an abstraction, and it could be enjoyed—and most viewers unfamiliar with Javanese culture probably did enjoy it—simply as a plotless study in choreographic design.

Nine women slowly entered. There were two groups of three dancers each, the three other women walked alone. As the dancers swayed gently, taking careful steps and gesturing delicately with their hands, patterns gradually formed and shifted. A program note explained that when the nine dancers were neatly arranged in three rows, they represented the union of all aspects of the human soul with their grouping. But the moment could also be savored for its compositional balance, proportion, and serenity.

Advances and retreats by the women were symbolic enactments of events from the story of *Arjuna's Wedding*. Yet they, too, could be appreciated simply as beautiful steps in space.

MARCIA B. SIEGEL[8]

The sacred dance form *Bedhaya* was the one most readily recognized by the American audience for its pristine classical expressiveness, despite the fact that the nine majestic women did almost nothing that resembled any dancing familiar to us. Swaying from side to side or gliding smoothly forward on their toes, they maintained a very still, inward concentration. Their

7. "Javanese Cultural Riches Revealed," *New York Times* (21 September 1990). Reprinted with permission.
8. The first excerpt is from "Rare Glimpse of Javanese Dance," *Christian Science Monitor* (23 October 1990). The second is from "Steps Out of Time," *New York Press* (2 October 1990).

linear floor patterns dissolved from one cryptic design into another, almost as if something outside the dancers' will had caused each change. Heads tilting from side to side, hands curling or flicking back the ends of their scarves, they seemed to be gently brushing away any speck of dust that might cloud their aura of spirituality.

We walk into the performance area, which looks like a Little League ball field rather than a theater. That's okay. In Indonesia, you get to the *kraton* (the sultan's palace, where this dance originates) by burrowing through back alleys and fending off marauding vendors who crowd the dusty outer courtyard. The dance transports you out of whatever mundane trips you've had to take to get there.

They've set up high three-sided bleachers around a platform just wide enough for the large gamelan, about twenty-five instruments all spread out and facing different directions. There are carved and gilded low xylophones and tuned bowls, with hanging gongs, drums, flutes, the two-stringed Arabic rebab, and the singers' section up front. There's a wooden canopy over them, but not over the front two-thirds of the platform, where the dance will take place. The dancers must feel horribly exposed.

The gamelan is playing as we enter, and the anticipation I've been feeling all day rises to the surface. . . . The performance goes beautifully. First, *Bedhaya*, a stately ritual in which nine women move slowly together up the steps and across the stage, swaying and curving in occult formations, then continue off when they've completed the rite. Totally focused inward, with their fabulous costumes and headdresses, they remind me of some great, glistening ship that sails across the horizon, so far away and silent that it might have been a mirage.

PAUL PARISH[9]

The marriage of Arjuna to the Celestial Maiden is, from what I can understand, the origin in myth of the royal family of Yogyakarta and the basis for many of the most important rituals of the court. The most important court ritual is the sacred dance called the *Bedhaya*, in which nine women dancers reenact the marriage of Arjuna. The dance looks a lot like the temptation of Arjuna by the celestial maidens [in the dramatized version we saw the night before]: nine women perch and flit like birds. Their feet flick at the hems of their skirts while their hands weave like flowers in a light breeze and tease out the folds of the dappled veils that hang at the front of their skirts. In the middle of this dream, characters begin to emerge, and before it's over there are twisty daggers being twirled with astonishing skill and darted in mock combat. Dancers are impersonating Arjuna and the ogre, but the same atmosphere of trance prevails through to the end, though it came to a climax when the two main dancers [playing Arjuna and Supraba, the Celestial Maiden] presented their wrists to each other.

It awakened fantasies of becoming someone's blood brother. One woman stretched out her wrists and waited as the other approached and covered them with her own.

ALLAN ULRICH[10]

The balmy air of the Arboretum was filled with the enchanting sound of the magnificent twenty-five-member Javanese gamelan orchestra, with the gentle timbre of zithers, bronze gongs, metallophones, and other percussion instruments (all playing within restricted pitches) creating a near-magical spell. The only criticism lay in the use of amplification for the singers. They occasionally seemed overbalanced.

---

9.   "The Court Dance of Java," *Daily Californian* (21 September 1990).
10.   "Java Dancers Dazzle L.A. Fete," *San Francisco Examiner* (1 September 1990).

Classical Javanese dance stresses symmetry and group co-hesion over individual expressions of temperament. And as the nine women mounted the platform stage in costumes that featured long skirts, gold belts, and enormous pink-feather headdresses, one felt transported not by the exoticism of their dance, but by its universality.

Feet curl, bodies glide by imperceptible means across the stage, torsos bend slightly, the trajectory is slow and almost sculpted, dancers assemble and reassemble in patterns. Their gazes are not so much averted as fixed on some distant, enigmatic point. The number nine holds certain symbolic value in Javanese culture, and the T and grid formations are spun silkily in space.

NICOLE PLETT AND BARBARA FIGGE FOX[11]

Glistening with gold bracelets, headdresses topped with pink plumes, and gold-braided red tunics, the nine dancers enter in two lines. With unhurried care, each slowly advances one foot, shifts weight, and gently sways to that side, repeating the process in exquisite unison like a boat ritually rocking on some heavenly sea.

In Western dance, this might be compared to the entrance in *La Bayadère*, where each dancer follows in a line, repeating an extending movement until all have entered. But where the ballet dancers stretch in arabesque, the Javanese dancers have an inner focus. Their faces show no change; every movement of the downcast eyes, every tilt of the head, every articulation of the flexed wrists and circling fingers is prescribed.

In former times perfection in performing this dance was a matter of life and death. It reaffirms the power of the sultan by depicting the union of earth and sea, of male and female, of the sultan and his spiritual wife, the Sea Goddess, and it is

---

11.   "From the Pacific, Jewels of Java," U.S.1 (Princeton, NJ) (12 September 1990).

rehearsed only on certain days of the month and performed only at the anniversary of the sultan's coronation. It was said that the Goddess might return from the sea, inhabit the body of one of the dancers, and take her back to the sea.

Some of this feeling is evident even now, for to this day, Javanese know not to wear the color green at the beach for fear of being carried off by the Sea Goddess. And although the sons and the daughters of the sultan are among the royal relatives who perform Javanese court dance, no daughter of a sultan can risk being one of the nine *Bedhaya* maidens.

In the sultan's palace, this dance would last for two or three hours, and so hypnotic is this slow procession that it seems like hours until the dancers reach center stage. Though they continue to move slowly, they punctuate the adagio with flourishes of their dance scarves, red sashes at the waist of their long, slender sarongs. Almost imperceptibly they change formations, moving between positions with minute, tiptoe steps.

At some points they sink to the ground, and when seven of the women are poised—not seated or kneeling but somewhere in-between—two dancers, representing opposites of the soul and will, flick small leather daggers in a ritual conflict without contact. The conflict is resolved in a harmonious balance that signifies a unity between earth and sea, between will and soul.

Thus a ritual combines art and religion and the power of the state with the aim of inner peace.

June Vail

Arlene Croce, dance critic for *The New Yorker*, prefaced a 1990 review of Mark Morris' choreography with a denunciation of "the latest buzzword" from academia, "multiculturalism," which she defined as "the political advocacy of other than Western (or non-'Eurocentric') forms of dance."

"Those of us who are educated in the theatre may well wonder what there is to be political about," she continued.

> Multiculturalism exists and has always existed in American dance; there is scarcely an American choreographer of note who has not been influenced both by the pluralism of our society and by the way dance just naturally soaks it up. Pinning a label on a simple phenomenon like that is something only an academic would want to do. And only political academics would want to isolate the elements of pluralism in such a way as to aggrandize some and stigmatize others.

> The multiculturalists who cite recent trends in immigration have a case. There may be a need to promote the accessibility of Asian, Hispanic, and African dance companies, many of which lead a marginal life, with few bookings. But the dance forms themselves are hardly inaccessible—they're part of every dance tradition the West knows. At their purest (assuming that one can find village and street

◄ *Indrani in Bharata Natyam pose, photo by Habib Rahman*

festivals that are uninfected by television and tourism), they still speak a rhythmic language intelligible to all who love dance. To argue otherwise fits in with certain divisive notions of culture popular in the universities; it also fits in with theories of curriculum reform.

But the discussion of multiculturalism among dance people has a peculiar urgency. What the academic partisans of Asian and Hispanic and African dance are really telling us is that ballet is in decline and the creative impetus in modern dance has finally petered out; therefore, we'd better pay attention to these other styles or we have no dance to talk and write about. The key word is "other" (it's another buzzword); the assumption is that these styles lie outside the mainstream and are kept there by mainstream prejudice. And what the pols want (and, given their weight in academic quarters, seem certain to get) is the creation of special-interest groups that need special-interest, academically fostered insights in order to be understood.[1]

Croce's perceptive—but, in my opinion, outmoded—remarks draw a line between artists and sensitive viewers, on the one hand, and politically motivated academics on the other. They assert that dances can be intuitively, universally understood. They assume that "high art"—that is, Western theatrical dance—stands apart from and above "folk art."

It is not uncommon for dance criticism, consciously or not, to confront the dances of other cultures with assumptions such as these, derived from Western performance

---

1. "Multicultural Theatre," *The New Yorker* (23 July 1990), 84. © 1990 Arlene Croce. All rights reserved.

conventions. Indeed, during the past twenty-five years, dance criticism has focused primarily on describing, analyzing, and evaluating theatrical dance forms—modern and ballet—as works of art "on their own terms." From the perspective of at least one prominent New York critic of this period, dancing's relation to political climate, trends in the other arts, or the choreographer's intentions was "feature story fluff" extraneous to a dance review. Journalistic dance critics tended to think of their skills as personal ones, derived from a breadth of dance-viewing experience, analytic insight, and literary craft. The notion that such personal skills were also culturally shaped had not gained common parlance.

But more recently a generation of dance writers familiar with the work of anthropologists such as Clifford Geertz, Joann Kealiinohomoku, Adrienne Kaeppler, and critical theorists such as Michel Foucault, Julia Kristeva, and Roland Barthes have reconsidered the nature of criticism. Feminist theory, literary criticism, and experiments with ethnological fieldwork report-age have caused many dance writers to reflect on both writing and movement as cultural performance.

An American critic encountering non-Western dance tradi-tions cannot avoid the cultural, sometimes political, dimen-sions of viewing and reviewing dance events. Writing about world dance raises questions about the historical or spiritual significance of unfamiliar movement forms and our ability to grasp them.

Clearly, perception and understanding—the prerequisites of description and evaluation—lie not merely in the indi-vidual beholder's eye, but also in the beholder's culture. Multiculturalism brings dance writers face to face with our own cultural construction. The challenge is to become aware simultaneously of the values that mold our critical commen-tary as well as those that shape the choreography. To describe what we are viewing and interpret its significance, responsible critics must consider how we see—what we habitually look for and what we ignore—and how we report it.

Self-aware dance writers can choose ways of using language that focus not just on dances but on the interactive nature of dance events. We can become more conscious of how we tend to view and review performances—what we look for and what we report. Our reviews can highlight theatrical impact, performers' skill, choreographic forms, and social meanings. In addition, we can regulate our focus to pinpoint performance details or encompass an entire dance event, including our own culturally influenced response, the way a flashlight beam can be adjusted from a narrow ray to an expansive wash.

To examine some specific ways American critics have watched world dance, I pored over a box of clippings collected by Sukanya, an internationally recognized Indian classical dancer whose unlikely home base is an island near my home in Maine. With her mother, the even more renowned Indrani, she had gathered articles from 1960 to 1987 during biennial tours of the United States in a program titled "Classical Dances of India." The thirty-four reviews and features in Sukanya's collection cover dances in Bharata Natyam, Orissi (also known as Odissi), and Kuchipudi styles, performed at venues ranging from a Lincoln Center gala to a school assembly in Bangor, Maine. The authors, many of them established critics, represent national and regional newspapers such as the *New York Times*, the *Washington Post*, the *Los Angeles Times*, and the *Boston Globe*. College and small-town papers such as the *Skidmore News* and *New Haven Register* are represented by student reporters and "lifestyle" writers.

Setting articles by experienced and inexperienced dance writers side by side, without regard to positive or negative evaluations (Sukanya assures me that all reviews are included), provided me not only with a gold mine of information but also with a fair random sample of journalistic styles and points of view over a twenty-year period. Through a close reading of the texts, I set out to examine the patterns and habits—good and bad—that American critics reveal in their work. Which aspects of an Indian dance performance do critics notice most? Which words recur most frequently? And how do the structures of our reviews (yes, one of my own is included in the sample) reflect our critical perspectives?

To assist in analyzing the reviews, Dr. Ronald R. Smith, my colleague at Indiana University, entered them as continuous text into a computer, using the Oxford Concordance text-analysis program. The resulting printouts yielded an alphabetical list of words and phrases, in decreasing order of frequency, and indicated their use in context. Not surprisingly, the computer search and my interpretive readings indicated that the focus of many of the reviews matched the approach most American critics bring to modern dance and ballet.

All the reviews, for example, describe Indian dance's theatrical impact: visual impressions of the choreography, colorful costumes, sensuous perfumes, and candlelit effects. Since Indian temple dancing has been recreated in the twentieth century as a theatrical form, the descriptive emphasis seems appropriate. But most accounts offer surprisingly little specific detail:

> The captivated audience was struck at once by
> the very opulent costumes with their brilliant
> colors and fine silks.[2]

Descriptive adjectives abound. Some of the most frequently used are: *beautiful, ancient, complex, human, intricate, clear, dramatic, fine, young, precise, cultural, excellent, delicate, exotic, feminine,* and *vivid.* Such adjectives convey general impressions and may indicate a writer's enthusiastic or bewildered response, but they do not communicate what the performers actually looked like, or precisely how they moved.

2. Vicki Duncan, "Indrani Captivates BSC Audience," *The Bowie* (*Maryland*) *Blade* (25 September 1975).

Describing unfamiliar movement is challenging, for the codified gestures of classical Indian dance offer a striking contrast
to the signs and symbols of Western dance traditions. Depictions of choreographic effects range from the laboriously
abstract—"The dances themselves were complicated arrangements of motion calling on all parts of the body for optimum
effect"[3]—to the metaphoric—"Indrani and Sukanya are also
skilled actresses—with every mood passing over the face like a
thunderburst or a radiant sunbeam."[4]

Only about half the reviews note the articulation of the
body in Indian dance, offering impressionistic description of
dance poses and movement with varying degrees of success.
Among the most frequently used nouns in the collected reviews are *feet*, *eyes/eyebrows*, and *hands*:

> Just about everything moves in Indian dance.
> From quivering eyebrows to stamping feet,
> whatever can be articulated usually has been
> many centuries ago and, moreover, codified
> into an intricate expressive vocabulary.[5]
>
> □
>
> There are . . . an almost endless variety of
> minutely calculated gestures for eyebrows,
> fingers, and the neck, all parts of the body
> usually left to their own devices in our ballet
> and modern dance forms.[6]
>
> □
>
> Indrani struck a delicately asymmetrical pose
> in imitation of the god with knees bent, one
> foot arched, and the opposite hip thrust side-
> ways, and hands raised beside the mouth as if
> holding Krishna's emblematic flute.[7]

3. Anne Hillerman, "Classical Dance Offered," *New Mexican* (30 October 1975).
4. Anna Kisselgoff, "'3 Generations' Is Indian Family Affair," *New York Times* (1 October 1979).
5. Lewis Segal, "Indrani at Schoenberg," *Los Angeles Times* (22 May 1979).
6. Christine Temin, "A Delicate Touch from India," *Boston Globe* (25 July 1978).
7. *Ibid*.

A lack of knowledge of the history and vocabulary of classical Indian dance limits detailed description, analysis, and evaluation. In portraying the theatrical impact of these performances, many reviews employ Western dance as an aesthetic point of reference, which can be helpful. But habitual modes of perceiving and writing, used without self-awareness, tend to reduce the event to a safely exotic novelty.

Most of Sukanya's reviews, from both metropolitan and small-town papers, spotlight the personalities of the performers. Their danced portrayals of superhuman, magical beings create an aura of exoticism that perfumes their offstage as well as onstage presence. The apparent similarity between American ideals of feminine beauty and the bearing of Indian classical dancers invites comparison with princesses and goddesses. The metaphors can be more or less lavish:

> They both had a fairy tale aura—Indian goddesses beckoning the audience.[8]
>
> □
>
> Few there are who possess the divine touch and even fewer there are who can represent the dance of a given country so that the very soul of the land involved is captured in their art. . . . Who can better interpret the consorts of the gods than a seemingly living goddess in the person of Indrani?[9]

This idealization corresponds to the elevation of ballerinas to star status.

Many reviews compare Indrani and Sukanya on the basis of their physical beauty, age, and technical mastery. But none of these reviews compares the duo stylistically with other classical Indian dancers. Nor do the majority of reviews situate the dancers within a historical or spiritual tradition.

---

8. Martha Jane Opitz, "Indian Dancers Dazzle Quietly," *Poughkeepsie Journal* (17 March 1981).
9. Jennie Schulman, "Indrani and Sukanya," *Backstage* (3 December 1982).

However, more than half of the reviews do refer to certain program notes on Indian dance and culture. Concert programs used the term "pure dance" to differentiate dances that do not tell a story from narrative ones that do. I understand the term "pure dance" to mean harmonized gestures of the hands and arms and curves of the body that interact with rhythms and cross-rhythms of the feet to create a complex flow of movement. The term reappears in many reviews, but in different guises, like the whispered phrase in a children's "telephone game":

> Most of the dances combined movements which remind an audience of mime with what could be called "purer" dance forms.[10]
>
> □
>
> At this stage of her career, Indrani seems content to appear as a dance actress rather than the vivid pure dancer we have seen in the past.[11]
>
> □
>
> Here she luxuriated in the purity of movement, movement for its own sake.[12]

These examples raise questions about the educational role of dance reviews. Imprecise explanations can obscure or trivialize complex concepts or aesthetic structures.

If background is helpful only when accurate, the same holds true for analysis of the dance form itself. For example, here are some of the "rules" of classical Indian dance, transmitted in the collected reviews:

---

10. Hillerman (30 October 1975).
11. Anna Kisselgoff, "Dance: Indrani and Sukanya Offer Three Indian Styles," *New York Times* (16 November 1982).
12. Robert H. Newell, "Indian Dances Superb," *Bangor Daily News* (1 December 1977).

Sukanya in Orissi pose, photo by Habib Rahman

> In Bharata Natyam, the dancer bends the waist;
> the Orissi dancer bends the hips.[13]
>
> □
>
> The pattern is to begin simply and progress through increasingly complex rhythms while the tempo accelerates accordingly.[14]
>
> □
>
> Another set of "rules" are the rhythms which consist of a 3-beat, 4-beat, 5-beat, 7-beat and 9-beat, all compacted into eight beats of music.[15]

As laid out in these three explanatory examples, the perceived "rules" are not only confusing but incorrect. What shape would a classical dancer who bends at the hips, but not at the waist, be forced to maintain? The intricate rhythms and textures of Indian music do not uniformly progress from simple to complex and from slow to fast and cannot be "compacted into eight beats of music." These examples suggest how difficult it can be to translate unfamiliar and sophisticated forms of dance and music into accessible English.

But if a critic is not an authority on a non-Western dance form, why should potential ticket-buyers bother with a review? What would make it worth reading? I have thought about the dilemma of the nonexpert critic in terms of my own journalistic writing and offer three possible solutions.

One option is to become an expert, and establish critical authority as a scholar, observer, and participant. This alternative may be more practical for some writers than others. Certainly it would be difficult to become an expert on more than a few of the world's dance traditions.

---

13.   Judith Galligan, "At the Dance: Classical Rhythms of India," *New Haven Register* [no date].

14.   Mary Sullivan, "Classical Indian Dance Offered at Belfast Concert by Sukanya," *Courier-Gazette* (Rockland, Maine) (August 1980).

15.   Kathleen L. Edwards, "Dancer Brings the Magic of India to Maine Audience," *Portland Press Herald* (4 August 1980).

Within this "expert" mode of criticism the most thought-provoking review in Sukanya's collection interprets the performance by clarifying the simultaneous religious and erotic nature of classical Indian dances:

> In this respect, Sukanya was breathtaking in her first two Orissi solos, exuding the strange and captivating sensual languor of this style, so close to the erotic temple sculptures that India has made famous. With one hip curved, with every deep plié sunk into with deliberation, with every expression conveying both desire and purity. . . . For, as Indrani showed so often, these are essentially love dances. The subject of adoration is God himself in human form. The erotic desires expressed by the dancers are desires for union with the divine.[16]

The proposition that dancing can be simultaneously pure and sensual, erotic and divine, is mentioned only this once in thirty-four articles. Several reviews comment that although classical Indian dance derives from temple dancing, it is "surprisingly" unsolemn. They seem to assume the mutually exclusive nature of religion and sensuality. Many reviews allude to the dancers' voluptuous qualities with metaphors of fluidity and sexuality, such as "flowing movement impregnated with symbolism," and references to sinuousness and feminine charm. Some additional descriptive terms include *immaculate control, intense exoticism, mystery,* and *excitement.*

However, the coincidence of spirituality and seduction in the repertory performed by Indrani and Sukanya challenges Western assumptions about the antagonism between religion and dance. Unfamiliar with the spiritual wellsprings of Indian classical dance, most critics did not look for evidence of divine

---

16.   Kisselgoff (16 November 1982).

and earthly love and perceived only the most literal panto-mimic references to religious themes. Accordingly, the most commonly used nouns refer to aesthetic characteristics (*style, mime, beauty, costume, rhythm*); the second most frequent suggest emotional states (*love, emotions, expressions, joy, moods*); and the most rarely used refer to religion (*gods, demon, temple, prayer*).

For the less knowledgeable writer, a tempting alternative to actually becoming an expert is to pretend to be one, using information gleaned from press releases, program notes, and other sources. This approach has been called "cheating" by Javanese critic Sal Murgiyanto: "A dance critic starts cheating when he writes as if he knows what he does not know."[17]

A third option, more practical and honest, is to experiment with ways of writing that do not insist on the authoritative, factual tone that journalistic conventions tend to encourage, but that generate lively, internally coherent, thought-provoking, and often self-reflexive commentaries.

A critic avoids cheating by realigning her critical stance from that of "expert" to the more self-aware "interactive observer." When necessary, she concedes unfamiliarity and refers to authorities. For example, one college reviewer interviews local experts, quotes program notes, and cites the performers' own commentary. Reflecting on her own expectations and partial knowledge, she articulates the criteria underlying her evaluations. A dance writer might well explain, for example, the reasons for asserting that Indian music exhibits "astonishing fluency." Since judgment implies comparison, the candid critic appropriately answers the question—compared to what?

To my mind, the most engaging writing among Sukanya's clippings frankly admits inexperience and conveys delight in encountering a new art form:

---

17. "Seeing and Writing about World Dance: An Insider's View," DCA *News* (Summer 1990), 3.

I went *expecting* to be slightly baffled by the intricate rhythmic structures, the specific gestural meanings and the sacred historical tradition of the dances from India.[18]

□

I came away *feeling* as though I had seen a Fonteyn.[19]

□

In the same way that I *assume* someone unfamiliar with ballet would be able to tell instinctively that Suzanne Farrell was a fine dancer, so *it seems* obvious to an *inexperienced* Westerner than Indrani and Sukanya are fine performers in another classical style.[20]

[Emphases mine.]

These examples also demonstrate the use of the pronoun "I": I *went*, I *came away*, I *assume*. Personal pronouns counteract the usual authoritative tone.

However, a personal approach can also be misused to validate the "truth" of eyewitness testimony instead of straightforwardly presenting one interpretation among several possible ones. Conventional journalese transmits "truth" and maintains the critic's authoritative position as "correct." Most of these reviews conform to this style of writing. A striking feature is that the most frequently used verbs are *is*, *was*, *are*, and *were*. A factual tone conveyed by excessive use of the verb "to be" could be altered by using verb forms such as *may, might, could, seems*, or *tends* to help convey more provisional perceptions.

The computer text analysis program reveals that, among all verbs used more than once, the thirty-four articles contain

---

18. Galligan [no date].
19. Laura Shapiro, "A Standing Ovation for Indrani," *Boston Evening Globe* (20 October 1975).
20. Temin (25 July 1978).

only two verbs conveying specific actions or movement qualities—*flow* and *sashay*. The reviews tend to talk about dancing without actively evoking it, possibly because world dance forms are hard to see when we do not know exactly what to look for.

Since we tend to see what we have been trained to see, can uninitiated audiences understand foreign dance forms except in culture-bound terms? No, they can't. Do most viewers want to? Probably not. But in print, dance critics have an opportunity to describe dancing in ways that can help readers understand our own culture as well as the one embodied onstage.

Generally, Americans' familiarity with the art of non-Western cultures has expanded since the 1970s, although this sample of reviews does not demonstrate dramatic changes in perspective over time. Is the current interest in world dance driven by a politicized "multiculturalism," as Arlene Croce's article suggests? Is it the result of changes in America's ethnic mix? Does world dance, appetizingly packaged and displayed, merely cater to the American public's thirst for novelty? Does it signal greater awareness and respect for human diversity or merely indulge our nostalgia for "the family of man"?

The expanded audience for world dance may indicate all of the above. But beyond demographics, political correctness, and feel-good exoticism, the concept of multiculturalism suggests a way to redefine critics' relationship to all forms of dance, including even the most familiar.

Multiculturalism helps us to conceptualize non-Eurocentric traditions *and* Western theatrical forms within a broad spectrum of possibilities for human movement, spanning history and cultures. The term "world dance" implies that all dances are ethnic, including our own. And as dancing comments on, rejects, creates, or maintains particular social or aesthetic norms, in a particular time and place, so does critical commentary. Critics are ethnic, too. Watching world dance sometimes means watching ourselves.

ARTICLES

ANDERSON, JACK, "Sukanya," *New York Times*, 25 January 1987.

CUNNINGHAM, FRANCIS, *Dance Magazine*, November 1979.

DUNCAN, VICKI, "Indrani Captivates BSC Audience," *Bowie Blade* (Maryland), 25 September 1975.

DUNNING, JENNIFER, "Classical Indian Fare," *New York Times*, 17 November 1985.

EDWARDS, KATHLEEN L., "Dancer Brings the Magic of India to Maine Audience," *Portland Press Herald*, 4 August 1980.

ENDTER, ELLEN, "An Indian (from India) Finds Maine a Fine Place to Dance," *Maine Sunday Telegram*, 5 November 1978.

————, "Sukanya's Dance Provides a Glimpse of Indian Culture," *Times Record* (Brunswick, Maine), 15 November 1979.

FLAGG, PAT, "Sukanya Entrances Kids, Adults With Indian Dances," *Ellsworth American* (Maine), 1 December 1977.

GALLIGAN, JUDITH, "At the Dance: Classical Rhythms of India," *New Haven Register*, c. 1973 [no date].

HACKETT, MARILYN, "Sukanya: She Sashays Out ...," *Lewiston Journal* (Maine), 29 May 1980.

HILLERMAN, ANNA, "Classical Dance Offered," *New Mexican*, 30 October 1975.

HUNT, MARILYN, *Dance Magazine*, February 1980.

KISSELGOFF, ANNA, " '3 Generations' Is Indian Family Affair," *New York Times*, 1 October 1979.

————, "Indrani and Sukanya Offer Three Indian Styles," *New York Times*, 16 November 1982.

LEVY, SUZANNE [CARBONNEAU], "Sukanya's Indian Dance," *Washington Post*, 29 March 1982.

MCDONAGH, DON, "Dance: The Art of Indrani," *New York Times*, 5 April 1973.

————, "Indrani and Troupe Perform at Hunter," *New York Times*, 3 February 1968.

MARTIN, JOHN, "From India: Indrani, Ragini Devi's Daughter, in Debut," *New York Times*, 7 August 1960.

NEWELL, ROBERT H., "India Dances Superb," *Bangor Daily News* (Maine), 1 December 1977.

NUCHTERN, JEAN, [no headline, dance section], *Soho Weekly News*, 1 October 1979.

OPITZ, MARTHA JANE, "Indian Dancers Dazzle Quietly," *Poughkeepsie Journal*, 17 March 1981.

PATEL, NARENDRA, "Indrani and Her Dancers and Musicians of India," *Dance News*, November 1975.

PEARSON, ALLAN, "East Indian Duo: Refinement, Grace, Beauty," *Sante Fe Reporter*, 17 May 1979.

SCHULMAN, JENNIE, "Indrani and Sukanya," *Backstage*, 3 December 1982.

SEGAL, LEWIS, "Indrani at Schoenberg," *Los Angeles Times*, 22 May 1979.

SHAPIRO, LAURA, "A Standing Ovation for Indrani," *Boston Evening Globe*, 20 October 1975.

SULLIVAN, MARY, "Classical Indian Dance Offered at Belfast Concert by Sukanya," *Courier-Gazette* (Rockland, Maine), August 1980.

TEMIN, CHRISTINE, "A Delicate Touch from India," *Boston Globe*, 25 July 1978.

TUCKER, MARILYN, "Frogs and Fish and Demons Too," *San Francisco Chronicle*, 3 November 1975.

[UNSIGNED], "Hindi Dance Group Debuts at Regent in 'Dance of Joy,'" *Skidmore News*, 23 October 1975.

[UNSIGNED], "Queen of Heaven" (Central Park Performance), *Newsweek*, c. 1968 [no date].

[UNSIGNED], "Superb Sukanya," *Express* (Trinidad/Tobago), 17 August 1984.

[UNSIGNED], "The Dancer Never Retires," *News & Cine India*, 5 October 1979.

VAIL, JUNE, "Learning to See Our Own Ethnicity," *Maine Times*, 22 April 1983.

Deborah Jowitt
Joan Acocella
Marcia B. Siegel

: LOOKING OUT: Perspectives on Dance & Criticism
Multicultural World. David Gere, Ed. Prentice-Hall
ng to Grips with the 'Other'"   *1995*

DEBORAH JOWITT: "Coming to Grips with the 'Other'" implies labor, a buttocks-clenched stance in the theater, with eyes wide and brain pumped up to catch every shred of cultural significance. Is this what is required of the conscientious critic? That is the issue that we're going to address: how we fire up with notions of the Other in the course of a working night in the theater, or a session at the keyboard, or in the shower, where I tend most often to ponder my values and desires.

Everything outside myself is Other, but some Others are more alien than other Others, and familiarity often comes on little cat feet where we least expect it. During a 1990 performance of *Golek Menak* by dancers from the Javanese Court of Yogyakarta, there was a point when the warriors began to dance in the *gaga*, or rough masculine style. I suddenly felt something run along my legs and realized that some of their movements were similar to what must have been a bastardized version that I had performed regularly for over two years with a pan-ethnic company called Mara and Her Legends of Cambodia. Mara had told me that there was a Javanese step in our piece, and that was it. And so that was mine, that step.

◄ *Matachine dancers, Jemez Pueblo Turquoise Clan, New Mexico, at the 1990 Los Angeles Festival, photo by Don Bradburn*

I think, in cross-cultural reviewing, that far worse than ignorance (which has its uses) is condescension. And condescension, whether intentional or unknowing, often brings with it a
kind of willful disregard. I have a collection of such reviews.
There's Winthrop Sargeant in *The New Yorker*, reviewing the
Kerala Kalamandalam performing Kathakali at Hunter Play-
house, saying that "there was no expression on the faces of
most of the participants. Either that or their make-up is so
heavy I cannot imagine facial expression is possible."[1] He is
speaking of a tradition in which acute intricacies of facial
expression are part of the dancer's training. And he ends by
saying, "One gathers that rural Indian audiences are vastly
thrilled by these doings. I found it all technically fascinating,
but just a trifle long drawn-out."

Or take Mel Gussow, in the *New York Times*, reviewing Peking
Opera at Alice Tully Hall and saying, "It doesn't have the
universal appeal of such brilliant Japanese theatre as Kabuki
and Bunraku. Undoubtedly, its interest is largely for students
of Oriental art and for those who cherish it as part of a revered
tradition." And then he goes on to say that:

> the simplistic narratives put an undue em-
> phasis on letters, both purloined and incrimi-
> nating. In the climax of one play, Mr. Chu
> copies one such document onto the apron of
> his robe, a gesture whose meaning remains
> obscure. However, the reaction of the charac-
> ters to these missives is unflaggingly melo-
> dramatic in the manner of early silent movies.[2]

If Gussow had been paying attention either to the program
notes or the performance, I think he would have noticed that
the character was writing on his sleeve because he needed the

---

1. *The New Yorker* (5 December 1970).
2. *New York Times* (14 August 1981).

information the letter contained and because the letter was about to be destroyed.

However, I also tried to look at reviews of Western dance from other countries to see if that would help clarify our own cultural biases. I have, for example, a few reviews written in the 1970s by critics in India about Dan Wagoner's company. I found that the critics were eager to understand and to display, somewhat timidly, their sophistication about Western dance, and the reviews touched me very much by their good-heartedness and their openness, even when I, as a Western dance expert, started at occasional misperceptions and misinformation.

There are some odd things in these Indian reviews, but no odder than our reviews might seem to an Indian. Critics think of their audience when they write, and about what their audience knows. Wrote one critic:

> And if what was going on had little to communicate, especially to those fed on Indian dance styles like Bharata Natyam, it had to be remembered that the lack of wide communication is precisely the strong point of art that breaks away from the conventional. While somebody exclaimed at the recital that he would any day prefer to see a third-rate Bharata Natyam recital, another saw common points between what he saw and some indigenous games and dances that feature some local processions. There was too much of squirming and contortionist movement, another thought.[3]

But the critic went on to say that in terms of body and movement control, the performers combined the strong points of the "athlete and the circus artiste with an elegant dance

3. *The Hindu* (25 January 1974).

sense of their own." Another critic said, "[A] poet sitting by my side remarked that the dances of Dan Wagoner reminded him of the poetry of Meeraji, or at best they resembled the new experiments of prose-poetry which are raising raging controversy in Urdu literature."[4]

In every way these writers were seeking to make something that they felt was a little foreign accessible to their readers by comparing it to familiar things. In a way, the allusions critics here or in India may use are not demeaning, because it comes down to the audience for whom you are writing, and that's crucial. As critics we can't be bootstrap ethnologists. Assuming such a stance only burdens our prose and alienates our readers and, anyway, the few real ethnologists would snort at what we said because we couldn't possibly come up to snuff in a short time. To consider, and deal with, the possible puzzlement of your imagined general public is to acknowledge that you have the same cultural heritage—that you are one of them. References that facilitate understanding seem to me justified.

However, I realize that I take for granted who my audience is. One time in Denmark I was asked to write a review of a Bournonville ballet for the big Copenhagen daily *Politiken*. I sat down at a borrowed typewriter in a hotel room and went into my usual deadline mode, a little bit tenser than usual. Then I thought, "Oh my god, I'm writing about Bournonville for the Danes! What am I going to say?" Because at home, I'd say something like, "All of you who know this style and who've never seen A *Folk Tale* (because it hadn't been shown in the United States at that point), have you got a treat coming! And listen, it's like this, and there are these incredible, incredible trolls. ..." But I couldn't write that way, and it took me an agonizing time in a foreign country on a deadline to try to figure out how the hell to start. I couldn't use a narrative mode

4. *Morning News* (Karachi) (3 January 1974).

and tell the story, although maybe not all Danes know it; so when I talked about the plot I could never say, "Junker Ove takes the goblet from the girl Hilda, whom he supposes to be a troll, and spills its poison on the ground, where it bursts into flames. You can't imagine the stagecraft they have at the Royal Theatre." I had to say something to the effect of, "*When* Junker Ove takes the goblet from Hilda (which you know perfectly well, being Danes) …" and then go on. I had to use language differently.

The Other sometimes surprises me. I wrote a review of Ritha Devi, the Indian dancer, when she first came to the United States and was very surprised and gratified to get a letter from her saying how nice it was to have me talk about form and movement style, because in India, she said, all the critics talked about were her hennaed palms and her jewelry and her flowers and her flashing eyes. On the other hand, as a white critic in America, I have occasionally been brought up short when writing about what is often advertised as "Black Dance." In one case, I attended a program advertised as "Classics of Black Dance," but that turned out not to be true; there were very few classics on the program. One dance, whose title I don't remember, featured a very fine young male dancer, and at one point he appeared in a blue satin loincloth with a red flower at his crotch and in a somewhat incomprehensible dramatic dance did what I was ill-advised enough to describe as "wiggling" or "wriggling." It was not a serious African-derived pelvic movement.

In response, I got a letter from a black critic-choreographer telling me how she thought I was demeaning the dancer. I thought I was criticizing the *choreographer* for demeaning the dancer. I had to show the letter to a colleague who was black to try to find out what I had done. I hadn't thought of anything at this concert as Other. This was American modern dance as I knew and sometimes loved it. Now I felt I had to be more guarded.

I offer these as examples of how the Other is not always identifiable to us. We think we know a lot about an art form, and it turns out we offend someone. On the other hand, it can turn out quite well when we write about something we think is foreign to us.

"Criteria" is a word that comes up a lot, but it's one that I'm uneasy with. We all have values that are part of us and that we don't fully understand, while to me a criterion means that you've set something up consciously for yourself. I don't approach things from the point of view that, "I have these criteria. Does the performance measure up?"

I think that criteria can get in the way. For instance, there's no reason to suppose that one should find a Japanese folk dance as rich as an elaborate kabuki spectacle. One wouldn't expect a Neapolitan folk dance and Bournonville's *Napoli* to offer the same kind of experience. But it's only when I imagine, or when we imagine, that they *should* that we really get into trouble. Especially when we feel guilty or defiant for preferring one to the other and are then unable to understand or appreciate what we're seeing. I can't watch the Matachines dance and pretend that I'm one of them. I can research their traditions. I can sharpen and use the tools that I have—my eyes, my ears, my sensibility, my ability to make sense of my perceptions, my language.

When I look at a dance, something inside me is at work, assessing the experience: "This is what this is. It isn't this. It isn't that. I shouldn't be comparing it to that. It is this *thing* that I understand imperfectly, but that I respect (if it's worthy of respect, and there are things that are not)." If I use those tools, then I can deal as honorably and courteously with a culture that is not mine as I would deal with a guest in my own house.

JOAN ACOCELLA: I want to address what Deborah described as guardedness, and I want to speak in very practical terms, as Deborah did, about what one actually does at a concert. Something that we should take a look at is our personal values about what is beautiful and interesting in art. All people, all critics, have such values, and those values, by definition, are sentiments of preference. We are preferring one thing to another thing. Even multiculturalism, the philosophy that I have heard advocated so frequently for the sake of its presumed elimination of the injustice of preference, is a sentiment of preference. It is an attitude of preferring pluralism, radical pluralism, to the kind of aesthetic agreement that people in most societies take for granted and hold dear.

Specific aesthetic preferences are often firmly expressed—even by people who regard themselves as multiculturalists. Take, for example, what have been described as the jazz-influenced virtues of Balanchine's style of ballet—the fluid spine, the pelvic freedom, the syncopation, and above all the through-line in the dancer's musical response—all of which, I agree, derive in part from jazz. But for those who point to and celebrate these African-inspired influences in Balanchine's work, this jazz spirit is not just a neutral quality. Rather, it inspires pride and admiration, as an African kind of beauty. I love it, too, and I see it not just in Balanchine's company, but in American ballet in general. By now it is almost the American style of ballet. You see it in Miami; you see it in San Francisco. And if you love it, you will love less the things that are its opposite, such as the Cecchetti style, which is more vertical and more decorous, and which minces things rather smaller and finer. You will probably also have some doubts about the Kirov Ballet's current style, which is very end-stopped and, in my opinion, musically sluggish.

So you will hold some artistic or aesthetic experiences closer to you, and other things—different things—you will see as more remote from you. You may feel the desire to consult indigenous people regarding appropriate criteria for evaluation, but such consulting can only take you so far.

Apparently the Kirov ballerina most beloved of the Russians is Galina Mezentseva, a dancer whose virtues are lost on many American ballet critics. We have consulted Russian people as to their criteria for evaluation, and they tell us they love Mezentseva because she is "expressive." Expressive. We see her clawing the stage and making terrible facial expressions, and the Russians tell us this is expressive. No, after a while, because we love dance—love certain things about it— we have to make our own decisions on the basis of that love, and take responsibility for the decisions.

How do you do this in a reviewing situation? Recently I went to see an African heritage group called Ko-Thi, an excellent group from Milwaukee, and I had what I would call the paradigmatic multicultural experience. I watched these wonderful dancers and drummers, and realized as I sat there watching them that for me there was something missing. My heart hungered for something that wasn't there. I don't think this was my first thought, but it was my second.

What I was hungering for, as I quickly realized, was Aristotelian form. This is a Euro-American value: art as a parabola, with a beginning, middle, and end—a certain kind of shape, with a certain complication in the middle. I missed something else as well, another deeply held Western value: what I would call Mozartean development, in which a germ of an idea is expressed and then it is worked upon, in different ways. Certain threads are pulled out, certain threads are sewn in; the idea is expanded, contracted, fiddled with, made more and more interesting. You take a long journey with it, and when you get to the end, you say, "Ah, this is what they meant at the beginning."

So as I was watching Ko-Thi, I was missing these two things. But I said to myself, "Well, they're not trying to do these things. What are they trying to do? What is the kind of beauty or interest that is being presented to me here, insofar as I can divine it?" I didn't have an ethnomusicologist next to me to consult, but what I decided was the beauty being offered by Ko-Thi was vertical layering rather than horizontal development—that the real interest of the show lay in polyrhythms. This was the party I had been invited to. The complication and richness that for me are absolute values in art were there, but in a different form from, say, that of *Oedipus Rex*.

And there were other things there. There was richness in the different timbres of the instruments. There was richness in the dynamics and attack of the dancers. But above all the source of beauty was rhythmic, and once I plugged my plug into that socket, or what I imagined to be that socket, I was able to engage in what I consider a pretty authentic act of evaluation and see what there was to love in Ko-Thi. I believe, however, that the reason I was able to plug into that socket was not that I'm so liberal-minded but that the value in question is one that I already hold. Because I'm an American, African artistic values are already part of my values. I don't think we can see beauty that we haven't in some measure been taught to see.

I grew up in Oakland, California, and went to public school. Black dance and black music were part of my childhood. And when I watch Ko-Thi, what I see is related to that. Black dance belongs to me in the same way that *Moby Dick* belongs to black teenagers in American high schools. There are other things that don't belong to me as much as this, and I care for them less.

Alastair Macaulay, in his remarks on classicism in Javanese *Bedhaya*, mentioned repose and said that this was a value for him. I think Macaulay can stand a lot more repose than I can.

He is English and I am American. Similarly, there are national differences in artistic values among critics as in other things, and if we don't take our values as seriously as we take the press kit, we are going to end up with what I call "genteel reviews." A lot of the programs at Asia Society in New York seem to me to get genteel reviews. You know the kind I mean, "Oh, wasn't that an interesting gourd he shook?"

We do this kind of reviewing, I think, when we are nervous. Or I do. I know, because I can see it in my clippings. When I'm nervous about reviewing something that is unfamiliar to me, I have a tendency to write a kind of dilettantish review, a let-me-count-the-ways review. "Oh, what wonderful costumes. They were red, they were blue, they were green. Oh, what wonderful dancing. There was jumping, there was hopping, there was turning." This is a genteel review, a UNICEF review, one that expresses an uncomplicated pleasure in seeing something different. It is not criticism, which is an analytical act, an act of capture and understanding.

I think you have to follow your values even at the risk of saying things that seem narrow-minded. Earlier, Hanay Geiogamah mentioned a reviewer in Glasgow who had said of an American Indian Dance Theatre performance, "Oh God, those drums go on for so long." Ridiculous as this seems, I don't think it's an illegitimate statement. That reviewer should get out of the business, or at least out of the business of reviewing Indian dance, but it's not an unfair statement. What I do find unfair was the other critic's statement, also mentioned by Geiogamah, that American Indian Dance Theatre wore an inauthentically large number of feathers. I don't believe in second-guessing as far as authenticity is concerned, but if drums bore you, or if you think Peking Opera is not as interesting theatrically as bunraku or kabuki, it is fair to say so. The answer to insufficient understanding is assimilation, but there's only so much we can assimilate. Some things will still look foreign to us, and I'm not worried about that. I'll just keep on attending all these concerts, and I'll bring to them my American values—that is, my Euro-Afro-American values—and try to act like a human being. I don't believe in *"Tout comprendre, c'est tout pardonner"*—that if you're wise enough, you'll like everything equally. Nobody likes everything equally, and to say you do is to write false criticism.

MARCIA B. SIEGEL: I think actually that I'm a little bit more intimidated by what Joan just said than I usually am in going to see some dance I've never experienced before, because she's articulated the view of criticism as aesthetics. I don't see criticism quite the way Joan expressed it. I don't see it as looking for what I love, in the first place, and I'm sure that means that my writing is not as aesthetic or poetic as Joan's often is.

I try not to be judgmental, and I try not to look at anything with those kinds of things in play: what is beautiful, what is the best, what is ideal, all those things. I even try not to deal with whether I love it or not, though I hope that always comes across. Allegra Fuller Snyder has said something that I think is very profound and very applicable to what I'm trying to do: it's the idea that, as an ethnographer always discovers, the material begins to reveal itself.

The dance is my best information. The dance itself. And my observation of the dance—which, in a sense, is my participation in the dance—allows me to connect the performance with my writing. The rest is background. What that means is: Look at the dance. I've heard very little about looking at the dance—how to look at the dance, how to find out what's in the dance—for yourself.

The first thing people these days start to complain about is the assumption that some artistic universals exist. I'm very unsure about universals. I do know that physicality is univer-

sal. And it underlies all performance, certainly all dance performance, and it contains basic information. I am fully aware
that physicality always takes place in reference to a context
and that the context is not universal. I'm not telling us to
ignore the context—use every bit of context that you get—but
I'm sorry, we don't get very much context. We don't get it from
program notes; we don't get it from press releases. We get
information in the program notes and the press releases about
the music. But the dance itself, nobody tells us how to look at
it. Since we're not experts in every one of the world's cultures
ourselves, in the end, we're really out there on our own. When
we critics confront the performance, all those bits of information may not even apply to what we're looking at specifically.

So I'm just going to talk about movement elements that are
loaded with information to which I think we really don't pay
enough attention. I am Laban-trained and I certainly believe
that a lot of the information in Labananalysis and in
Choreometrics is useful observation information. It gives us a
lot of data about dynamics, about the use of space and time
and weight, about the use of phrasing, and about the way the
personal expression comes out. Choreometrics is a detailed
look at body use, the body parts that are used, the spatial
orientation, the transitions, and the shape of the movements. I
believe there are a lot of interpretive problems with
Choreometrics—for example, I don't subscribe to the value
judgments that are placed on the categories—but the creators
of Choreometrics did come up with basic tools that would help
us if we went back to the coding sheets and the information.

But I would say that all of the Laban systems—Labanotation,
Labananalysis, Choreometrics—though they are probably the
largest body of really analytical work anybody has ever done
with movement, are Eurocentric. Laban theory is centered on
the body and looks at movement from the performer's point of
view, not from the audience's point of view. It doesn't really

concern itself with choreography and with the overall form of a dance piece or the process of a performance. It doesn't address the group. It leaves out a lot of things that aren't paramount in Western choreography. So even though it's useful, I don't find it is everything. I'm going to just suggest a few other things that I've been working with, and that seem to get more at the whole experience of some form of dance which is unknown to us.

☐ The first one is *lexicon*. That is, look at the whole thing and see the things that are used the most. Any things—body things, spatial things, costume things—anything that is an essential to the vocabulary of that particular dance. The beat and rhythm are essential. I don't see how you can look at almost any dance form without understanding what its rhythm is and how that rhythm is expressed—how the dancers express it, how the music expresses it, how those two form a whole. Certainly the Matachine dances, if you looked at them in terms of the form or the steps, you might say, "That's just repetition. They're doing the same thing over and over again and it's too simple; it's just boring." But in fact rhythmically it is complex, it is polyrhythmic. It's hard to count that, and it's hard to see how the dancers relate to the musicians, and that to me is what is fascinating about it and what makes me want to know more about it.

☐ *Orchestration*. How do the parts of the dance go together? How do the individuals go together with the other individuals, the dancers with the music? How are all of the parts of the piece orchestrated together? We in the West tend to see dance as a unitary entity, where everything serves one choreographic end, or is meant to be in one form—Aristotelian, if you will. Not all dance is like that, and we should discover what the orchestration is, how it works, what it serves. What are the segments in the dance, and how are they marked off? What are the changes, who signals them, and how does the dance change? These are all things that occur, nonverbally, and are never told to us in advance. But we can see them.

☐ *What are other structural elements?* For example, is it a progression or is it just a series of things that are on an equal level all the way through? How is this structure or progression communicated? Is there a leader, as there is in the Matachine dances? Who dictates when things change, and what does he or she dictate? The music, the dance? Is the sequence learned on the spot? Is it spontaneous or is it learned ahead of time and always repeated the same way? Those are structural elements.

☐ *What is the performance practice?* Is it filled with artifice and how is artifice stated and where does it come from? Or is it very naturalistic? What are the focus patterns? In the Javanese *Wayang Wong*, the focus of the noble characters is down and always down, it's never out to the audience. These are performance practices that we can see in front of us.

It seems to me that we can't even begin to come to grips with the Other until we start looking at these and many other aspects of specific dances. And never mind how interesting it is for us, what a rich experience it is for us to uncover and deal with all of these elements! It's just a constant learning experience for me to work that way. One's awareness is growing larger all the time as you bring these things to the surface.

The last thing I'm going to say is that movement analysis is not criticism. It just gives you information. And there are many other skills a critic needs. Deborah mentioned some and I would say there are maybe four that are the most important. One, at the top of the list, is empathy. E*mpathy.* And I actually think that getting into movement and understanding movement from various perspectives is the way that you empathize. Since Deborah is a dancer, she's done some of those steps, so she empathizes, or has a kinesthetic reaction because she can dance those. I'm not a dancer but I often feel empathy with performers because I'm with them on a movement level.

The second of the four is sensitivity and judgment in selecting and collating from among those movement and other elements that you've observed and taken in.

Third is acquiring and accumulating background information and applying it appropriately. Everything from what you've read and what you've seen in the past and all of your travel and all of the performances you've ever gone to and reviewed successfully or unsuccessfully constitute your background. Plus all of the information you can get from other people and from the people who do it.

And finally, the ability to write and describe. That is a whole other set of skills and practices in itself.

GROWING UP MULTICULTURAL

Mark Morris
interviewed by Joan Acocella

JOAN ACOCELLA: You're a good person to ask about multiculturalism, since you've absorbed so many traditions into your work. I see you, in a way, as a paradigmatic American choreographer, in the sense of picking up a multitude of influences, influences that are reflective in some measure of the ethnic mix in our country. If I'm not mistaken, it was at a Spanish dance concert that you received the *coup de foudre* and decided to become a dancer.

MARK MORRIS: Yes, I was something like eight and I saw what then was a fabulous company, José Greco and Nana Lorca. My mother took me. It's when I knew what I had to do immediately. So I started studying with a woman in Seattle, Verla Flowers, who turned out to be a fabulous, generous dance teacher who gave me a great deal of room to grow up and learn to dance. So the first things I did were flamenco and *escuela bolera* and *jota*. From there I got hooked into a very bad group of people who did primarily Balkan dances, mostly Yugoslav, Macedonian, and Croatian-Serbian, and a lot of Bulgarian stuff. That was really the first time I performed a lot. That was also the first time that I had to sing and dance on stage and do things that were, I guess, foreign.

A video performance of "O *Rangasayee*" was shown during this interview.

◄ *Mark Morris in "O Rangasayee," photo by Lois Greenfield*

ACOCELLA: You also danced with a Russian group.

MORRIS: Yes, the very first appearances I think I made dancing were with this little balalaika orchestra at the Russian Center in Seattle with this ancient, ancient man who coached me and convinced me to do things dancing that I would now regard as too dangerous. Every Sunday we would get together, there would be a concert, and I would clear some music stands and dance around. As for ballet, I started when I was ten or eleven, but I was never very interested until a little bit later, fifteen or sixteen or something like that.

ACOCELLA: Let's get up to age seventeen. You went to Spain.

MORRIS: I went to Spain. I did the thing that a lot of people do as teenagers, which is leave high school early and discover Europe with a Eurailpass and a backpack. My intention was to go all over and do all sorts of things. I ended up spending a month in Skoplje, Yugoslavia, and hanging out and going to weddings and stuff with several people who were sort of important choreographers in Yugoslavia and Macedonia. And from there I went all over Spain. I lived in Madrid for about six months and studied with several people. I started with very intensive flamenco things: one day would be castanet class, the next day only feet, and the next day only turns—which was the day I usually skipped. I gradually converted to Jotero and studied jota for almost the whole time. I pretty much dropped flamenco by the end because I was really very disappointed in the way it was going, in the performances I saw and the way it was taught. The honeymoon was over. And of course Franco was still around and so it was ridiculous to live there. I knew then that I only wanted to do jota and flamenco if I stayed in Spain and lived there and became as Spanish as I could, and I realized that I couldn't do that. So I abandoned ship and moved back to the States and ended up in New York a little bit later.

ACOCELLA: What was it that you so much loved about Spanish dance, enough to consider living there?

MORRIS: I don't know, that's really hard to say. The flamenco thing was because I think it was basically a solo form, and it was very much a closed thing. It never really worked for me to watch it in performance so much. It did to watch it at parties and clubs. That was also the fun of dancing with Koleda [Koleda Balkan Dance Ensemble] in Seattle. You know, the best part was the parties after the show, when somebody would play a *gajda* [Yugoslavian bagpipe], and everybody would get drunk and dance a lot. It was fun. I know I'm not supposed to say that, but it was. That's why, in Spain, I switched over to full-time *jota* work, because it's all couple dancing and all group dancing and fun. Fun fun fun fun.

ACOCELLA: Let me take you to New York. You are there. Age nineteen.

MORRIS: It's very hot.

ACOCELLA: Yes, it's very hot. You move into a sixth-floor walkup on Second Avenue and Second Street with another dancer—Penny Hutchinson, your old friend from Seattle—and you go to work for the Eliot Feld Company.

MORRIS: Yes, my first job was a ballet job.

ACOCELLA: How long did the Feld gig last?

MORRIS: One-and-a-half years—it's a long time. I stayed a year and a half with everybody I danced with, almost exactly to the day. I danced with Eliot and then I danced with Lar Lubovitch and then I danced with Hannah Kahn on and off for a long time, which was great. And then I danced with Laura Dean Dancers and Musicians. But as someone who was starting to choreograph, it got very frustrating for me. When I was with Eliot, I was choreographing every second. When there was a break, I would make up a giant dance on the sidelines. And I don't know if it was because of the time or if it was a particular arrogance, but I started to see that everybody was stealing my steps and putting them in their dances.

ACOCELLA: And so you figured out it was time to become a choreographer yourself.

MORRIS: Yeah, sort of like that. I would just get impatient with how I thought a dance company should not be run, and of course, I would never do that when I started my own company.

ACOCELLA: You went to India with Laura Dean, right?

MORRIS: New Zealand, India, Indonesia.

ACOCELLA: What did you see in India?

MORRIS: I saw great great great dancing all the time. I would say that the thing that really knocked me out was a particular Kathak performance. It was in Delhi actually, and it was of course incredibly hot and the concert was incredibly long. But I was really excited because I felt like I *got* it. The whole thing was on a cement slab stage and I would follow along and I thought, "This is great." The dancer would do the rhythm and the musicians would take over. I'd listened to a lot of Indian music, but I hadn't seen a lot of Indian dancing. And then it got longer and longer, so after about an hour and a half I was, how do you say, *gone.* It was actually frightening for me. I can always keep track of rhythms, that's not a problem for me. But suddenly it was like, "OK, this is going to happen," and then it would go on and on and on and on and get more and more fabulous and more and more thrilling. And I ended up going back to the hotel and sobbing all night. It wasn't jet lag. It was really one of the greatest things I've ever seen.

ACOCELLA: In 1984, you made a solo that seems directly related to your experiences in India.

MORRIS: Yes, it's a dance called O *Rangasayee*, and it's to music by M.S. Subbulakshmi, who is my favorite singer ever. I worked for a very long time trying to decode the music to make it danceable for me. I figured out a complicated math system that helped me deal with the incredibly vast piece of music that it's set to. It's about twenty minutes long.

ACOCELLA: Could you talk about the musical challenges, the rhythmic challenges in the dance?

MORRIS: If you don't have a lot of experience in listening to Indian music, then you know it's gonna be rough. I knew enough about it to be able to tell when things changed and when variations were happening on certain phrases and just sort of the logic of it, from listening to the music. Because I love it. And, I don't know, it seemed to me that I should do a dance to it, so I had to come to terms somehow. But of course it's totally hard.

I think, if I had known more, I wouldn't have dared to attempt this dance. I always thought of it as a sort of homage. It's not just based on dancing that I saw but on, like, waiters in restaurants and lepers on streets. And how I felt. So it's very personal. It's not an Indian dance, certainly, and it was never intended to be. I could say that I like Indian dance just about better than any other dance I can imagine and, you know, it was a little too late at that point to start studying or join a convent or something and change everything. So I decided that I should do it from my own point of view, my own experience, in my own deep admiration and love of these forms. And that's why there aren't any direct quotations. Or I hope there aren't. But, you know, the dance is about things I like, and things I had never felt before. It seemed important for me to dance them somehow.

ACOCELLA: I wonder, do you think that being from Seattle made you more permeable to influence?

MORRIS: You mean than someone who's not from Seattle?

ACOCELLA: I mean, geography is a destiny of sorts, and when you're in Seattle you're in a place where many people from Asia have settled.

MORRIS: I would say that, for example, the whole time I was going to school there was a Samoan dance team, and there were lots of people who'd come from Hong Kong, and there were a lot of Cambodians and Vietnamese. There were lots of languages and lots of fashions going on at the schools I went to, and that, of course, was my favorite thing. It was great.

ACOCELLA: So it's not just those particular kinds of dance, but the fact that the sheer experience of foreignness is not so foreign.

MORRIS: I guess. It never seemed foreign to me.

ACOCELLA: Seeing something different from what you see in your own backyard. That's what I mean.

AUDIENCE COMMENT: Well, if he goes to school with Samoans and they're coming over after school, they're in his backyard.

ACOCELLA: That's right, and then it's not foreign, if it's in your backyard. But most of us don't have the entire world in our own backyard. You may have a bigger backyard than I do.

MORRIS: I think all that Joan's really asking is, Did I hide with all of my white friends or did I participate in the ethnic diversity which defines Seattle? And that's a lovely thing and it's easy to go crazy about certain expressions, but you know, come on, just lighten up.

AUDIENCE QUESTION: Can we go back to O *Rangasayee* for a minute? Were you interested in the physicality of the movement or was there another level that affected the choices that you made, and the images?

MORRIS: Well, that's a complicated question because, I mean, that question could be asked of any dance ever made. It's not like I just wanted to show some moves that I thought would get me a grant or something. What one is thinking when one is dancing is very often different from what is seen by other people. But I don't know, I can't really be more specific because it's, to me, it's close, it's very close to me. I don't have a dogma, I can't really defend it in any way. I can just say that it is a piece of music and a singer and like, you know, this is from lots and lots of music and lots of listening and lots of thinking and looking. And that's what happened.

ACOCELLA: Were you moved as well by the text of the song?

MORRIS: I found out what I could about the text, which wasn't very much. When I do pieces to music with text in any language, whether it's English or Italian or whatever, I either illustrate the text or I don't. Sometimes I don't because I don't have the resources to find out what is being said exactly, and I just deal primarily with what it seems to me is being said, from how it sounds.

ACOCELLA: Sometimes, when critics speak of influences on your work, they speak of attributes that are very easily identifiable as part of a different tradition—Indian ragas, Balkan dance forms, *jota*, or whatever. But I wonder whether the study of different musics, such as Indian or Eastern European, hasn't perhaps affected the deep basis of your thinking about dance, so that those influences will then come up in your most "Eurocentric" work.

MORRIS: Gasp!

ACOCELLA: No, no; for instance, L'*Allegro*. What I'm thinking is that—not to lead the witness too far—but that you might, from working with so many different musical traditions, and such refined and complicated ones, you might have learned a rhythmic flexibility or a rhythmic suppleness or a rhythmic curiosity, as it were, that would affect *all* your work.

MORRIS: I would say that the first time I even had to deal with difficult rhythms directly was when I was doing a lot of Bulgarian stuff, and you know that actually proved to be much more rich in a way than a lot of the Spanish stuff I had dealt with. I mean, it's a different approach to rhythm and it's now been broken down by everybody into, "This is in $^{11}/_{16}$." But it's actually just, you know, light and heavy. That's what it really is. And so when you dance, you're not counting as far as you possibly can to get up to eleven. The same with singing. Also, in dances before and after O *Rangasayee*, I used many more direct quotes from dances that I knew or dances I had seen and that I was, you know, ripping off some moves from. Then those experiences with different dance forms and different rhythms and different kinds of music just sort of became part of everything else that I know about.

ACOCELLA: So the whole gestalt changes. Everything shifts to accommodate the influence. I think that possibly all those different kinds of music might have been like a university of rhythm; when you graduate, you know what to do. Do you think that there would be certain kinds of foreign dances that Americans would feel more sympathy with?

MORRIS: I think in general American audiences would like something that's short and fast.

ACOCELLA: But you said you loved Indian dancing so very very much. You're a member of the American audience.

MORRIS: I know from viewing experience that Bharata Natyam is much easier for people to watch than Kathakhali, which either makes you go back every day because it's the best thing you've ever seen, or makes you run to the parking lot. The short-and-fast thing I said as a joke, but I also think it's true.

ON THE THRESHOLD OF A NEW DECADE

Guillermo Gómez-Peña

Los Angeles 1992: two thousand years of dreaming, five hundred years of nightmare. Frequently I wake up as a Mexican in U.S. territory, and with my Mexican psyche, my Mexican heart, and my Mexican body, I have to make intelligible art for American audiences that know very little about my culture. This is my daily dilemma. I have to force myself to cross a border and there is very little reciprocity from the people on the other side. I live an experimental life. I physically live between two cultures and two languages. I have a little *estudio* in Tijuana and one in San Diego, separated from one another by a one-hour drive, but also by one thousand light years in terms of culture.

Tijuana is partially industrialized, compact, rebellious, and extremely tolerant of otherness. San Diego is high-tech, spread out, ultraconservative, and xenophobic. The only features they have in common are their historical amnesia and the inevitability of their togetherness. When I am on the Mexican side I have a strong artistic connection to Latin American urban pop-culture and ritual traditions that are centuries old. When I am on the U.S. side, I have access to high technology and specialized information. When I cross back to Mexico I get immersed in a rich political culture, the postearthquake movements of political opposition. When I return to California, I am part of the intercultural thinking emerging from the interstices

---

This is an early version of material subsequently published in Gómez-Peña's *Warrior for Gringostroika* (St. Paul, Minn.: Graywolf Press, 1993).

◄ *Guillermo Gómez-Peña, photo by Jeffrey Scales*

of its ethnic milieus. I walk the fibers of this transition in my everyday life and I make art about it.

My experience is not unique by any means. Thousands of artists in the U.S. and other countries are currently crossing different kinds of borders and, as they do it, they are making a new kind of art. An art of fusion and displacement, an art that shatters the distorting mirrors of the much-touted Western vanguard. My story is only one among many and, by making art, I hope to contribute to a better understanding of the conflictive relations that exist between Chicano, Latino, and Anglo-American cultures.

PERFORMANCE

In April of 1492, Columbus departed from the port of Palos in three state-of-the-art *caravelas*: *La Pinta* for the prisoners, *La Niña* for the child molesters, and the *Santa María* for the religious fanatics. Columbus arrived in America without papers. Don't we all secretly wish he had been deported right away? In April of 1942, my uncle Pepe departed from Mexico City with one hundred pesos in his pocket. He arrived in Los Angeles without papers and became a clothing designer for prominent *pachucos*. Don't we all wish he dies in peace?

MEMORY

Mexico City is the postmodern city par excellence. Walking from neighborhood to neighborhood is like traveling from one continent to another, and vertically from one epoch to another. Pre-Columbian ruins coexist with colonial Spanish and neo–Classic French architecture. Houses built in different epochs during the past four centuries stand next to crystal skyscrapers hosting corporations and banks. Indian markets and video discotheques are at a walking distance from one another. And it all somehow makes sense.

Art is no less hybrid and involuntarily postmodern. The

sounds of regional folk music coexist on the radio with classical European music and rock-and-roll in both English and Spanish. On any given day, one can witness an Indian dance ceremony at the Zócalo and then walk to a nearby theater or gallery and attend an experimental art event. Despite all this, the official culture provides us with an idealized version of who we were (wholesome Indians) and who we are (modernized *mestizos*), which denies the acute syncretism of everyday reality. From Aztec to postpunk, all styles, eras, and cultural expressions are intertwined in this mega-pastiche called "El D.F." (Mexico City).

And those of us who grew up in such contexts developed what I call a vernacular postmodern sensibility. And cross-cultural fusion is at its core. This sensibility allows for the normal coexistence of drastically different cultures in our society and, in an art context, it favors sudden and even violent juxtapositions of images, sounds, and texts without demanding reconciliation or rationalization. Through the prism of this sensibility, past and present, pop culture and high culture, politics and aesthetics, rural and urban realities, pre-Columbian rite and Catholicism are perceived as logical dualities belonging to the same time and place. Most Anglo-Americans have to learn postmodernism as theory because their cultural experience is not marked with growing within and across a multiple-cultural strata. Their knowledge of Native American culture is distant and abstract and their attraction to black and Latino art is selective and temporary. In fact, the relationships that Anglo-Americans establish with their surrounding cultural others are either of sponsorship, messianism, or voyeurism, but very seldom of total immersion or dialogue. In Mexico, we are immersed in syncretism, and our survival skills to move laterally and vertically into the cultural Other are more developed. We have no other choice. The Other exists within us and multiculturalism is the very spinal cord of our personal and collective biography. It is only until we cross the border that we face the Other outside, thus becoming the outside Other for Anglo culture. When we cross the border our art becomes the double mirror that reflects this painful dynamic: Mexico in the U.S., the U.S. in Mexico, and us in between.

Performance

I clearly remember my birth. A major contradiction per se. A *mestizo* baby born in the Spanish hospital of the mostly Jewish quarter of Mexico City. Right between Virgo and Libra, as the church bells of a wandering St. Augustine were announcing the death of the day, I was being born from the contradictory lips of Marta, my beautiful mother, who worked in a Kodak shop at the time.

I remember the distorted reflection of my face in the metal torso of a Spanish soldier named Rodrigo. I remember the corpse of a viceroy in a window display of the financial district of Madrid. I remember the days Zapata and Villa entered the capital blessed with an almost mystical naïveté. Zapata performed by Brando and Villa by Telly Savalas. The same day my father brought home the first TV. I remember Batman, Mr. Ed, and Jungle Jim, the first Americans I ever met.

"Americans. *Que* weird," I thought.

The Border, the Fracturing of Memory and Identity

The 1960s in Mexico were also a decade of diaspora. Many experimental artists who felt suffocated by the inflexible structures of the official culture left the country in search of aesthetic freedom and spread throughout Europe and the United States. Ulises Carrión went to Amsterdam where he started an alternative space specializing in book art. Felipe Ehrenberg went to England where he cofounded the legendary Beau Geste alternative press and participated in the Fluxus movement. A decade later, my permanently unsatisfied friends and I departed, following the footprints of our older compadres. I chose California because I had always been more anti-European than anti-American and because I wanted to embrace the Chicano experience. A child of the Mexican crisis, I crossed the border in 1978 and something broke inside of me forever.

PERFORMANCE

September 1, 1978, Mexico City Airport. My best friends and relatives are gathered to say goodbye, *con mariachis y toda la cosa*. I am going to California, the other Mexico, and I don't know when I'll be back. As I cross the magnetic checkpoint, I turn and say to them: "I beg you to pretend I am about to die, this way you'll get used to my absence."

THE RUPTURE

Crossing the border meant much more than having to learn English or eat fast food. For the first time, I had to confront Protestant ethics, pragmatism, hyperindividualism, cultural deprivation, and racism on a daily basis. For the first time in my life I was truly alone and scared, without a family, a community, or a language. This abrupt confrontation with Otherness triggered many processes inside of me, the most obvious being the exploration of the conflicting relationship between my Mexican past and my U.S. present, my Latino-American identity and my new Chicano reality. Again, this process found its most effective and organic format in performance.

My early solo performances in California reflected the pain of the departure and indescribable loneliness of the immigrant. Once I spent twenty-four hours in a public elevator wrapped in a batik. I ended up being thrown into a trash can by the security guards. Another time, I brought my audience to the edge of Freeway 5 and screamed at the cars to stop and save me from shipwreck. When I was first busted by the

California police for looking suspicious, meaning, for being Mexican, my response was to do a performance in which I burned a photo of my mother while I screamed at the top of my lungs over the Los Angeles skyscrapers: "Mother bring me back to the Womb! Mother bring me back to the Womb!"

Performance gave me a vocabulary and a syntax to express the critical processes of rupture and transculturation I was undergoing, and through my performance practices, I was able to connect with others who were experiencing a similar drama.

PERFORMANCE

Los Angeles, 1989: *Noche de sorpresas y aficionados* at the Cabaret Babylon-Aztlan. "*Damas y caballeros*. Quiet please! Tonight we are proud to present an authentic, third-world performance saga with the working title 'A Mexican Heart in *Gringolandia*,' low-tech but filled with love, action, and violence, written, directed, and performed by El Charro-mántico *acompañado de su banda de* naked *mariachis*."

The audience applauds. El Charro-mántico says, "Thank you. Thank you."

You only know how lonely you are when you stand in front of so many lonely people. Shit. This part belongs to another script . . . but fuck, where the hell is that other script?

A MEXICAN LOST TRIBE

By coming to El *Norte* I paid a high price for my curiosity. I became part of a lost generation. As citizens of nowhere, or better said, of everywhere, we were condemned to roam around the foggy and unspecific territory known as "Border Culture." Today, a decade later, we still haven't been able to fully return. Despite the fact that I spend long periods of time in Mexico City, still write regularly for Mexican publications, and maintain a close dialogue with many artists and writers from "the center" (Mexico City), I am still referred to as "Chicano." The anthologies and festivals of Mexican culture rarely include my work because, "Guillermo, you live on the other side." And to live on this side still implies a form of betrayal. When I go back to perform or give a talk, I have to do it as a Chicano. My Mexican brothers have managed to turn me into the Other, along with the twenty million Mexicans spread throughout the U.S. Paradoxically, some Chicanos still have a hard time considering me a Chicano. Either I wasn't born in Aztlán, I didn't participate in the political struggles of the 1960s or 1970s, or I still have an accent that gives away my "Chilango" upbringing.

I have learned to not get hurt or waste my time demanding to be included in the nationalistic maps of Mexican or Chicano culture. I have learned to accept the advantages and disadvantages of being a border citizen, which means I am always the other, but I get to choose my identity. Depending on the context, I can be a Mexican, a post-Mexican, a Chicano, a Chica-lango, a Latin American, a trans-American, or an American in the widest sense of the term. One thing I know for sure: as a binational artist, my border identity is constantly shifting with my everchanging cultural topography. And the registers of this shift can be found in my performance and literary work. My identity, like that of my contemporaries, is not a monolith but a kaleidoscope. And everything I create, including this talk, contains a multiplicity of voices, each speaking from a different region of my self. Far from mere postmodern theorizations, this multiplicity is a quintessential feature of the Latino experience in the U.S.

PERFORMANCE

Hello, Raza? Can you hear me? I am standing right on the U.S./Mexico borderline, with a foot on each country, see, the line is actually bisecting my manhood. I've got a Mexican *huevo* and an American ball. And on top of that, I've got a poem for you. Check it out!

INTERVIEWER: "*Ici la radio publique* Montréal. September 23, 1989—by the way, he just turned thirty-four! How exactly has your identity been affected by your experience of Amerique?"

GÓMEZ-PEÑA: "Well, señorita, to be in America is a complicated matter. You are in relation to the multiplicity of looks you are able to display. Let me explain you better:

"I am brown therefore I am underdeveloped.

I wear a moustache therefore I am a Mexican.

I gesticulate therefore I am Latino.

I am horny therefore I am a sexist.

I speak about politics therefore I am a
  communist.

My art is indescribable therefore I am a
  performance artist.

I talk therefore I am. Period."

INTERVIEWER: "*Oh, c'est fascinant. C'est exotique.*"

GÓMEZ-PEÑA: "In order to multiply the perceptual readings of my identity, I always try to create interference during the broadcast."

THE BORDER IS . . .

"Border Culture" is a polysemantic term. Border culture means boycott, complot, *ilegalidad, clandestinad, contrabando*, transgression, binational; to smuggle dangerous poetry and utopian visions from one culture to another. But it also means to maintain one's dignity outside the law. But it also means hybrid art forms for new contents in gestation. Spray mural, techno-altars, poetry in tongues, audio graffiti, *punkarachi, video-corrido*, anti-Boleros, anti-*todo: migra*, art world, police mono-culture, an art against the monolinguist *tapados y ex-teticistas*.

But it also means to be fluent in English, Spanish, Spanglish, and Ingleñol, because Spanglish is the language of border diplomacy. But it also means cultural friendship and collaboration between races, sexes, and generations. But it also means

Gómez-Peña, photo by Jeffrey Scales

to practice creative appropriation, expropriation, and subversion of dominant cultural forms. But it also means a new cartography, a brand new map to host the new project, the democratization of the East, the socialization of the West, the third-worldization of the North, and the first-worldization of the South. But it also means a multiplicity of voices away from the center. Different geocultural relations among more culturally akin regions. Tijuana-Nuyo Rico, Miami-Quebec, San Antonio-Berlin, your hometown and mine; a new internationalism *ex-centris*. But it also means *regresar y volver a partir*—to return and to part once again. Border culture is a Sisyphean experience and to arrive is just an illusion.

But it also means a new terminology for new multihybrid identities, in a constant process of metamorphosis—social thinker, not bohemian; *accionista*, not performer; intercultural, not postmodern. But it also means to develop new models to interpret the world in crisis, the only world we know. But it also means to push the borders of countries and languages or, better said, to find new languages to express the fluctuating borders. But it also means experimenting with the fringes between art and society, legality and illegality, English and Español, male and female, North and South, self and other, and subverting these relationships. But it also means to speak from the crevice (the border is the juncture, not the edge, and monoculturism has been expelled to the margins). But it also means glasnost, not government censorship, for censorship is the opposite of border culture. But it also means to analyze critically all which lies on the current table of debates, even multiculturalism. But it also means to question and transgress border culture. What today is powerful and necessary tomorrow is arcane; what today is border culture, tomorrow is institutional art, not vice versa. But it also means to escape the current co-optation of border culture. But it also means to look at the past and the future at the same time. 1492 was the beginning of a genocidal era. 1992 marks the beginning of a new era, American post-Columbina, *America sin fronteras*. Soon a new internationalism will have to gravitate around the spinal cord of this continent, not Europe, not just the North, not just white, not only you.

We are living a paradoxical moment. As the Soviet Union and Eastern Europe welcome structural changes in the realms of politics and culture, the U.S. withdraws into its old monocultural republican formula. While other societies are being led by utopian thinkers such as Mandela, Havel, and Gorbachev, we are being misled by narco-politicos like Bush and sleazy theocrats like Helms. What have we done to deserve this?

Art has become a highly symbolic territory of retaliation. Ultraconservative government sectors are determined to defund and censor noncommerical art depicting sexual and racial alternatives to male WASP culture. McCarthyism is back, and again artists are being blacklisted and being labeled obscene, pornographic, and un-American. In the 1950s there was the Hollywood 10, in the 1960s, the Chicago 7; now we have the Art World 5 or 10 and many more to come. Nothing new, really. Censorship and panic politics have been at the core of U.S. culture since its inception. What surprises more is the intensity of the response in a moment where the rest of the world is engaged in reform and pluralism. This time censorship is part of a much larger political spectrum. Symptoms of a fascist state, the logical progression of a decade under the Reagan-Bush administration, are being felt everywhere. The attempts to dismantle affirmative action and bilingual education, the failed efforts to ban the right of women to practice abortion, the current militarization of the Mexican border, the unwillingness of the government to respond to AIDS and homelessness, the euphemistic war on drugs, and the illegal invasion of Panama are different expressions of the same censoring mentality, and fear of Otherness is at its core. We must not lose this perspective—any artist or arts organizer who believes in and practices civil rights, cultural pluralism, and freedom of expression is a member of a national resistance. And her/his words, images, dances, and actions are expressions of the zeitgeist of America.

We all are citizens of the end-of-the-century society. As the 1990s unfold, artists must conquer a central role in the making of this society. We must fine-tune our roles as citizen diplomats, border philosophers, and activists for gringostroika. We must practice, promote, and demand tolerance, dialogue, and reform. We must speak from the new center, not the old margins, and we must do it in large-scale formats and for large audiences. We must challenge the anachronistic myth that as responsible artists we're only meant to work within "ethnic" community contexts or marginal leftist venues. Our place is the world in crisis and our communities have multiplied exponentially.

Another important issue haunting our consciousness is the need to redefine the five-hundred-year celebration of the alleged "discovery of America." To participate in a project of redefinition is important to any group who doesn't feel responsible for the bloody European legacy on this continent.

Some people say that the 1990s will be the decade of the environment, but paradoxically, as my dear colleague Ellen Sebastian says, "We, the human beings, are the ultimate environment." We are the creatures in process of extinction and our ecosystems, the multiracial cities we inhabit, plagued by poor education, police brutality, and joblessness, are part of the nature we must save. These debates will inevitably point to the quest for a society beyond Columbus that truly embraces us all, including the multicultural and multisexual communities; the recent immigrants from the South and the East; the children and elderly people—our most vulnerable and beloved ones; the courageous AIDS carriers; and the home-less, whose only mistake has been not being able to afford housing. Contemporary art is already reflecting this quest and the government knows it. Unquestionably, U.S. society at the end of the century will be a fully borderized community, a kind of gigantic Brooklyn, or downtown Los Angeles. Demograph-ics, pop culture, and contemporary art can already testify in this respect. The first and third worlds have mutually pen-etrated one another. Multilingualism and multiculturalism are common practices in the artistic and intellectual milieus of this continent, and not because of status or fashion, but be-cause of a basic political necessity. To learn Spanish, English, and French and to study the history and art of our neighboring cultural Others becomes indispensable if we want to cross borders and participate in the drafting of the cultural and political topography of the twenty-first century.

There is no way around it: xenophobia, censorship, segregationism, and monoculturalism are expressions of a dying culture.

I try to imagine the future of art. Perhaps in the 1990s, artists and intellectuals will finally perform a central role in the public life of the U.S. Perhaps one of these days Amalia Mesa Banes will become Governor of California and Tim Miller the Mayor of Los Angeles. Perhaps Victor Hernández Cruz will be President of independent Puerto Rico and Chomsky will be Secretary of Information. Perhaps a multiethnic group of women artists will head a Ministry of Cultural Affairs. Perhaps there will even be a Ministry of Cultural Affairs with a budget equiva-lent to that of other, more civilized countries. Perhaps perfor-mance artists will be regularly heard on public radio and poets and philosophers will publish daily in the major newspapers. Perhaps events like the Los Angeles Festival will be televised by CBS. Perhaps there will be five cultural TV channels in every city and every important film and video art piece will be obtainable in the local Blockbuster video shop. Perhaps there will be so many alternative spaces that there won't be any need to call them "alternative" anymore. Perhaps, we will no longer need to imagine. But meanwhile, we must do everything we can to precipitate this change.

We must not just fight for funding without restrictions—we must fight for more unrestricted funding for many more artists from all cultural and sexual communities in the U.S. We must particularly promote and defend socially conscious experimental work that is articulating our present historical moment.

Performance

> I speak therefore I continue to be.
> Language my passport to your country
> language my journey to your arms
> language my most effective weapon
> language my two-way ticket to the past
> my abracadabra.
> A thread of life per sentence
> $10 a page
> postcard included.
> Life in America
> a cheesy TV talk show
> a color Xerox *fotonovela*.
> Stop.
> I am here to conflict with your plans.
> The future, compadre
> is not entirely yours.

San Diego, Two Years After the Fall of the Berlin Wall

I lie on the beach waiting for Christopher Columbus to discover me for the five hundredth time. It's October 12, midday, and the cameras are waiting like me. Televisa and CBS are ready to record history, or better said, to reinvent it. The fanfares of tourism are growing intense. My heart speeds up as my tongue goes physically crazy. . . .

But this time, Columbus didn't arrive. Spain and Italy were so busy fighting over credits that the entire production was postponed until 1999. I go back to the city to think of a better text to put into practice.

ON MULTICULTURALITY AND AUTHENTICITY

Marcia B. Siegel

There are a number of themes underlying our discussions about ways to approach world dance, and one of those themes is fear. In one form: fear of the Other. And I don't just mean racist fear. I mean that in Western dance many people think the business of a critic is establishing and protecting norms. To acknowledge high art in another culture is to threaten "our" standards (i.e., whatever it is we endorse to our readers). And it also threatens how those standards are determined, which is something we might look at for ourselves. Where did we get them from? What are they based on? How much do they influence what we write? If we open ourselves up to the Other, on equal terms, we'll have to give up our position as standard-setters, because it means acknowledging that someone else has set some other standard that's equally standard.

Another fear that I think is very active is a certain desperate need for criteria, which seems to me to be extremely Western. Critics are asking for formulas; we want everybody to tell us how to look at their particular culture. We seem to need these formulas quite desperately. We want to be responsible and not make mistakes. We have a certain mistrust of being on our own, confronting an immediate, unfamiliar experience, and dealing with it inside of ourselves.

A similar version of this article was published under the title "Looking at Dance from All Sides Now: On Multiculturality and Authenticity in Dance," *Ballett International* (July/August 1991).

◀ *Woomera Mornington Island Culture Team, Australia, at the 1990 Los Angeles Festival, photo by Janise Witt*

And then we have to think and be interesting in seven hundred words.

The matter of criteria is very problematic. For one thing, you can't always know what the criteria are. No matter how hard you try and how many people you consult, or even how many times you've seen the dance form before, you can't always know what that culture accepts as good or bad (if you're in the good-or-bad business).

And even if we could learn some of the basics of a culture, or of cultural forms, are we sure we know what the whole range is? Can we say that a performance we may see danced in Los Angeles is *the* Javanese court dance? Is this the only way to perform that dance or style? Is this the only context in which that style is seen? Everything from tourist performance to the most classical, private, and high-context high art can use these same kinds of elements—basics that are, in any culture, manipulated by and within the culture. We may see only one example of a dance in our lifetime, so how can we say we know which of its elements are seen across the culture and which are unique to specific genres or styles?

Western critics have hierarchies, though we may not admit it. Going from the bottom up, we pay attention to social dancing, pop dancing, jazz dancing, theatrical dancing, concert dancing, ballet. I actually left out a new form, which I think Jennifer Dunning very nicely established in 1990 in the *New York Times*: video dancing. But ballet dancing seems accepted as the crowning achievement of dance art in Western culture. And within that hierarchy, we also tend to respect old work more than we respect new work, and an "accurate" reproduction of an old work over a reinterpretation. Now, even if these hierarchies are justified and mean something (and I don't think they do), even if you were going to arrange dance by levels and categories, how the heck do you figure out the hierarchy in some other culture?

Another related fear is the question of establishing authenticity. When you travel, you realize what a huge variation there is, even within what seem to be the normative styles, of a given culture. Style, or technique, or form isn't just one thing. Although it may be ever so much simpler for us to identify a classical style or a folk dance form that someone has conveniently researched, it's folly to think that the form will remain the same, or has remained the same, for all time. I'm not even sure we can say the most meticulously researched and preserved forms *mean* the same thing for all time.

I do find the interplay between preservation and change, or what I think is the inevitability of change, both poignant and distressing. I also love old dances and I wish we could preserve old traditions and I know we can't. I think that is true in every single culture. It's true in ballet and modern dance. We've seen those two forms change drastically in the twenty-five years I've been writing. And that's right in front of our eyes. So how can we talk about "the tradition" or "the authentic" in a culture that may be thousands of years old and has been undergoing constant change over all those years—much of it instituted from outside, by colonial powers, and other kinds of influences?

Discussions among dance critics often concentrate quite a lot on "traditional forms." Those high-art traditions, those codified stage forms that are culturally endorsed—those are the things that tend to come to the United States on tour. The *Wayang Wong* is a good example. We're very lucky to have it, but it doesn't represent Indonesia. It doesn't represent Java. It's one form, and a very high-art, officially sanctioned, intentionally visible form. I don't think they're going to bring over some of the seedier forms, or some of the commonplace forms that people do in the backyard, which for me would be just as interesting.

The emphasis on traditional forms is easier for critics

because more writing and more analysis has been done about them—both their content and their manner of presentation. But these categories are changing, and they are complex and multifaceted rather than monolithic or static. I can't make that point too strongly.

We also have a great fear of making a mistake. We might say the wrong thing, and I must say that intimidating sanctions are often issued to critics and to presenters in discussions of "multiculturalism" or "world dance." I certainly take to heart everything I hear, but I am not going to be deterred from doing my work. And you shouldn't be deterred. Get the tools. Get the ability to look. Open your mind, and do it. Own up to what you're doing.

We are not anthropologists. We cannot be anthropologists. An anthropologist knows a culture deeply and goes there and studies it. An anthropologist tries to get direct information from the doers, from the culture itself. As critics, we'd like to have that, but we don't. We usually have access to the artists only through their press representatives and their presenters. We get little useful information from them. And even if we can get in direct contact and speak to the performers, the teachers, the choreographers, we have to surmount problems of language, problems of interpretation, problems of what is it that they really mean and do they understand what we really mean when we're trying to get this information. Again, I encourage you to be more confident of your ability to see and experience and feel things deeply. And to work, beyond that, on your skills, your descriptive and writing skills.

To me, being a critic is a great privilege because I can see a lot of things. I can address a lot of things. I can experience many different things. And I don't want to sacrifice that, as much as I may love other cultures and want to spend more time studying them. We just can't work intensively enough with any one thing to become anthropological experts. At the same time, we have to recognize and compensate as best we can for our personal biases and lapses in information. We can't go to see one performance of something and understand it. Mark Morris may have gone and looked at one Kathak performance for a long time and "gotten it." But what he got he translated into some personal expression. Our job as critics is to communicate on behalf of those performers, not to express our creative fantasies. If you think you got it, you can admit only to the limitations of what it is you got. But express that. Describe that. Address that. Don't just sort of say, well, this is it. I think we ought to have a little bit more humility about what it is we got.

Let's turn to the topic of multiculturalism, which is often confused with eclecticism. I don't think they're the same thing. Americans have long considered our culture a "melting pot," and, in that sense, eclecticism is not new. It's not new for a dancer to appropriate from other cultures. The whole twentieth century has been doing it, from Ruth St. Denis to Mark Morris. But recognize that when we're looking at their work, we're looking at a Western form, in which these elements have been inserted to make it more interesting, give it a twist, or pay an homage to something that the artist has been taken with. I submit that, although benign and well-meaning, this is nevertheless a form of cultural imperialism. No matter what Balanchine took from this culture and that culture, he still made ballet and we can recognize it as ballet. I'm not putting down ballet or Balanchine. I'm just saying, we should recognize that it's not multicultural, it's not intercultural. I am dismayed by Arlene Croce's idea that multiculturalism and all the imperatives that surround it are solved by the appropriation of any old culture's forms into Western forms. And that such an approach answers all our problems of conscience about recognizing the rest of the world. It doesn't for me.

Dance is more than that, and can be more than that. I don't

Eagle Dance, American Indian Dance Theatre,
photo © Jack Vartoogian

just mean that dance can have different colors or that it can have different cultural styles. I mean it can address other things, entirely, and still be wonderful, and still be worthy of our true attention and love. Western dance forms are built on individual creation, personality, the assertion of personal skills. They are theatrical, they are basically for a proscenium audience, for entertainment. All of that is great, but most of it is trivial and forgotten and just entertainment. Three-quarters of the world or more doesn't experience that, in their aesthetic or their dance forms. We in this country have almost no knowledge of dance as ritual, dance as a spiritual lesson, dance as a historical memory, dance as a means of communal bonding. And I could go on.

What this means is that you'd better get your newspaper to broaden its categories if it's still insisting that a critic can look only at ballet and modern dance. Political and economic realities are shrinking the claim these narrow mainstream arts can make on space in the arts pages. Work on your editors, and get them to see the expansiveness of nontheatrical spectator dance, participatory dance, ritual dance, and all kinds of other venues and forms. Even if there are no imported companies touring through town, the public festivals and entertainments of transplanted minorities and indigenous non-Anglo populations are part of every city's culture today. Can't we write about them as vibrant performance activity and experience? Isn't that at least as important to us as sitting in a theater and being constantly stunned with new tricks and new ideas?

I want to say something about fusion or appropriation, a piece of this puzzle that I think hasn't really been examined. Tourism and international exchange are everywhere—in our country, in Europe, in Asia, in Africa, all over. There's almost no place that's ten thousand miles from nowhere and hasn't been worked at by the artifacts of modern life. The world is getting smaller, for everyone. Information is not sacred.

Everybody shares information. Everybody appropriates everybody else's everything. And though I respect those beliefs and traditions that are coherent in other cultures, I also think that culture is becoming common property. And I think we have a real responsibility to attend to those problems of fusion, of tradition, of the ways in which forms are coming together, and of how they're changing each other. Creative work is coming out of that butting together, that explosion. In my view, that's where the new art is going to come from.

I admit that I am tired of Western culture. I think Western culture is tired; it's played out. Or at least this phase of it—ballet and modern dance as we've understood them are in a fallow period. We're seeing a lot of imitation, a lot of desperate clasping onto what remains of these older traditions, not very much "authenticity" of feeling, and certainly not very much creativity within those forms. And I admit that I'm not so interested in looking at or writing about the fiftieth reincarnation of these forms, although I don't expect to tire of Mozart or Balanchine, ever.

And, although Croce accuses those of us who have this attitude as being *mere* "anthropologists," I don't mind admitting that I have been interested in non-Western forms for a long time, almost from the beginning of my writing, and I find them more and more interesting, and more and more of a challenge. And what has emerged, very much to my surprise, is that the contemporary forms are really interesting—and they're not even forms. They're little things, peeking up here and there, from people who have not been totally stunned by the dramatic infiltration of ballet and modern dance training around the world, but have been able to assimilate them over a long period of time and have come to a resolution of "dance identity" for themselves. Or else they have danced out the colliding, still unassimilated elements of what contemporary life is for them. And I believe it's like a nuclear reactor, where things are bombarding up against each other and a surge of creativity is coming, or is happening. I personally want to be around to see that creative work, and to write about it, and I hope you'll be there with me.

JOAN ACOCELLA has written on dance and other arts for *The New Yorker*, *The New York Review of Books*, and the *Village Voice*. Her book *Mark Morris* was published by Farrar, Straus and Giroux in 1993.

JACK ANDERSON has been a dance critic for the *New York Times* since 1978. He is the New York correspondent for *The Dancing Times* of London and coeditor of *Dance Chronicle*, a journal of dance history. He is the author of six books of dance history and criticism and eight books of poetry.

ZOË ANGLESEY is a poet, translator, anthologist, and jazz critic living in New York. She edited the bilingual anthology *Stone on Stone: Poetry by Diverse U.S. Women*, published by Open Hand Books in 1994.

BRUCE FLEMING teaches English at the United States Naval Academy in Annapolis. He is the author of *Caging the Lion: Cross-Cultural Fictions*, published by Peter Lang in 1993.

BARBARA FIGGE FOX, a DCA member since 1977, is senior editor of U.S.1, a biweekly published in Princeton, New Jersey.

DAVID GERE is cochair of the Dance Critics Association, codirector of the Talking Dance Project, and teaches in the Department of World Arts and Cultures at UCLA. An ethnomusicologist by training, he lived in India from 1980 to 1982 and has written about dance as staff critic for the *Oakland Tribune* and the *San Francisco Chronicle*.

GUILLERMO GÓMEZ-PEÑA is a writer and experimental artist who was born in Mexico City and came to the United States in 1978. Since that time he has been exploring border issues, cross-cultural identity, and U.S./Latino relations through the use of multiple media. His *Warrior for Gringostroika* was published by Graywolf Press in 1993.

BRENDA DIXON GOTTSCHILD is Professor of Dance Theory at Temple University, Philadelphia correspondent for *Dance Magazine*, and coauthor of the revised edition of *The History of Dance in Art and Education*, published by Prentice Hall in 1991.

JUDITH GREEN writes about theater and dance for the *San Jose Mercury News*. She is a past member of the DCA Board and a long-time member of the San Francisco Bay Area's Isadora Duncan Awards Committee.

DEBORAH JOWITT has been writing on dance for the *Village Voice* since 1967 and teaching at New York University's Tisch School of the Arts since 1975. Her book *Time and the Dancing Image*, published by William Morrow in 1988, won the De La Torre Bueno Prize.

PATRICE CLARK KOELSCH is a professional philosopher by training and was the executive director of the Center for Arts Criticism in St. Paul, Minnesota, from 1985 through 1993. She is now a freelance writer, critic, and cultural worker.

SARDONO W. KUSUMO trained as a classical Javanese dancer at the Court of Solo. His current work is in a contemporary style that incorporates influences from Indonesian tribal dance. Sardono Dance Theater debuted at the Brooklyn Academy of Music in 1993.

ALASTAIR MACAULAY reviews theater, dance, and music for the *Financial Times* (London). He is the founding editor of the quarterly *Dance Theatre Journal* and, in 1988 and 1992, was guest dance critic of *The New Yorker*.

MARK MORRIS has created more than seventy works for the Mark Morris Dance Group since it was founded in 1980. In addition, he has created dances for many ballet companies and has worked extensively in opera.

SAL MURGIYANTO is a member of the dance faculty of the Jakarta Institute of the Arts. He has authored or coauthored five books on dance and the performing arts in Indonesia and recently earned his Ph.D. in Performance Studies at New York University.

PETER NABOKOV is Assistant Professor of Anthropology at the University of Wisconsin, Madison. His books include *Indian Running*, *Two Leggings: The Making of a Crow Warrior*, and *Native American Architecture*.

JULIA PARDOE (1806–1862) was an English poet, author, historian, and traveler. After accompanying her father, Major Thomas Pardoe, on a trip to Constantinople, she published a popular two-volume work on Turkey in 1837 that was reprinted three times.

PAUL PARISH is a dancer and writer who is the San Francisco Bay Area correspondent for *Ballet Review* and *World Ballet and Dance*. He writes regularly for the *Daily Californian* and the *Bay Area Reporter* and has contributed essays to *Noh Quarter*, a literary quarterly, and the San Francisco Ballet program.

NICOLE PLETT, a freelance dance critic and arts writer based in Princeton, New Jersey, is editor of *Eleanor King: Sixty Years in American Dance*, published by Moving Press, New Mexico, in 1988.

LEWIS SEGAL has been staff dance writer for the *Los Angeles Times* since 1984. He has viewed and often written about dancing in Greece, Denmark, Mexico, Guatemala, Chile, Peru, Japan, Korea, Taiwan, Thailand, Burma, Indonesia, Nepal, Bhutan, Cambodia, Vietnam, India, Easter Island, Rarotonga, Australia, Turkey, Egypt, Morocco, and Mali.

MARCIA B. SIEGEL writes on dance for the *Hudson Review* and is a member of the resident faculty of the Department of Performance Studies, Tisch School of the Arts, New York University. Her most recent book is *The Tail of the Dragon: New Dance, 1976–1982*, published by Duke University Press in 1991.

ALLEGRA FULLER SNYDER is Professor Emeritus of Dance and Dance Ethnology at UCLA. She has made a number of prize-winning films on dance subjects for which she received filmmaking grants from both the National Endowment for the Arts and the National Endowment for the Humanities.

R.M. SOEDARSONO is Rector of the Institute Seni Indonesia in Yogyakarta. He holds a Ph.D. from the University of Michigan and is the author of several books on Indonesian arts.

GUS SOLOMONS JR dances, makes dances, and writes about dances for the *Village Voice* and *Dance Magazine*. A frequent panelist, he teaches at New York University's Tisch School of the Arts.

VICKY HOLT TAKAMINE graduated as a *kumu hula* under renowned Hawaiian dance master Maiki Aiu Lake and teaches hula at the University of Hawai'i, Mānoa. She is coproducer of the documentary film *Kumu Hula: Keepers of a Culture.*

CHRISTINE TEMIN has been the visual arts and dance critic for the *Boston Globe* since 1978. She is a former member of the DCA Board and has taught dance technique and history at Middlebury, Wellesley, and Harvard colleges.

RICARDO D. TRIMILLOS is Professor and Chair of Asian Studies at the University of Hawai'i, Mānoa. An ethnomusicologist, he has conducted research on the music of the Philippines and Hawai'i, and popular/commercial music of the United States.

ALLAN ULRICH has been the dance critic of the *San Francisco Examiner* since 1980 and the newspaper's classical music critic since 1987. He also writes about dance and music for *Dance International* (Vancouver) and *Opera* (UK), among many other publications.

JUNE VAIL is Associate Professor and Director of Dance in the Department of Theater Arts at Bowdoin College in Brunswick, Maine. A former performer, she has written about dance for the statewide weekly newspaper *Maine Times* since 1982.

KAPILA MALIK VATSYAYAN is founding director of the Indira Gandhi National Centre for the Arts and has been involved in Indian arts administration for more than thirty years. She has authored fifteen books and innumerable articles stressing the interrelationship of the Indian arts. She holds the title Padma Shri and is a fellow of the National Academy of Dance, Drama, and Music.

ELIZABETH ZIMMER edits the dance section at the *Village Voice*. She has been writing about dance since 1973 for print and broadcast media in Halifax, Vancouver, Los Angeles, San Francisco, and New York. She is also an inveterate dance student and practitioner of contact improvisation.

JAWOLE WILLA JO ZOLLAR is the artistic director of Urban Bush Women. In 1992, the company received a New York Dance and Performance Award ("Bessie") for its collective work from *River Songs* through *Praise House*. In 1994, the company received the Capezio Award.

ALVERNO COLLEGE LIBRARY

2 5050 00826206 1

3-5-96

792.8
L863

REMOVED FROM THE
ALVERNO COLLEGE LIBRARY

Alverno College
Library Media Center
Milwaukee, Wisconsin

DEMCO